PEACHIE SPEECHIE'S

Speech Sound Handbook

Elicitation Tips, Visuals, and Word Lists for Speech-Language Pathologists

Written by Meredith Avren, M.Ed., CCC-SLP
Illustrated by Josh Avren

Speech Sound Handbook - First Edition 2022

Library of Congress Catalog Card Number Pending

ISBN 9798847403900
10 9 8 7 6 5 4 3 2

Published by Avren Books™

avren™ books
avrenbooks.com

PEACHIE SPEECHIE'S

Speech Sound Handbook

Introduction

This handbook was created to provide speech-language pathologists with clear visuals and simple elicitation tips to use with clients during speech therapy sessions. Articulation therapy has always been my passion, and I hope this quick reference guide will make eliciting speech sounds easier and more enjoyable for fellow therapists. The artwork was done by Peachie Speechie's graphic designer, my husband Josh. Together we have created what we believe to be a valuable tool for every speech-language pathologist, SLPA, and SLP graduate student.

This handbook is designed for ease of use. For each sound, the following is included:

- Mouth illustration to show placement
- Word list for practice
- Elicitation tips

On some pages, you will see a QR code. You can scan them with your smart device to access free speech sound production videos from Peachie Speechie's library. These videos can be used during therapy sessions or with parents during home practice.

SCAN ME

Thank you for reading this speech sound handbook. I hope you find it useful in your practice.

Sincerely,
Meredith Avren, M.Ed., CCC-SLP
meredith@peachiespeechie.com

Important disclaimer about this resource, Speech Sound Handbook: This book and the techniques presented in it are designed to be used by a speech-language pathologist. Users must use professional judgment and common sense when implementing techniques described in this book. Appropriate techniques vary based on the individual being treated. Some of the techniques suggest use of food/candies. Be sure to check for allergies and discuss treatment methods with caregivers prior to beginning therapy.

PEACHIE SPEECHIE'S

Speech Sound Handbook

Contents

Speech Sound Mouths

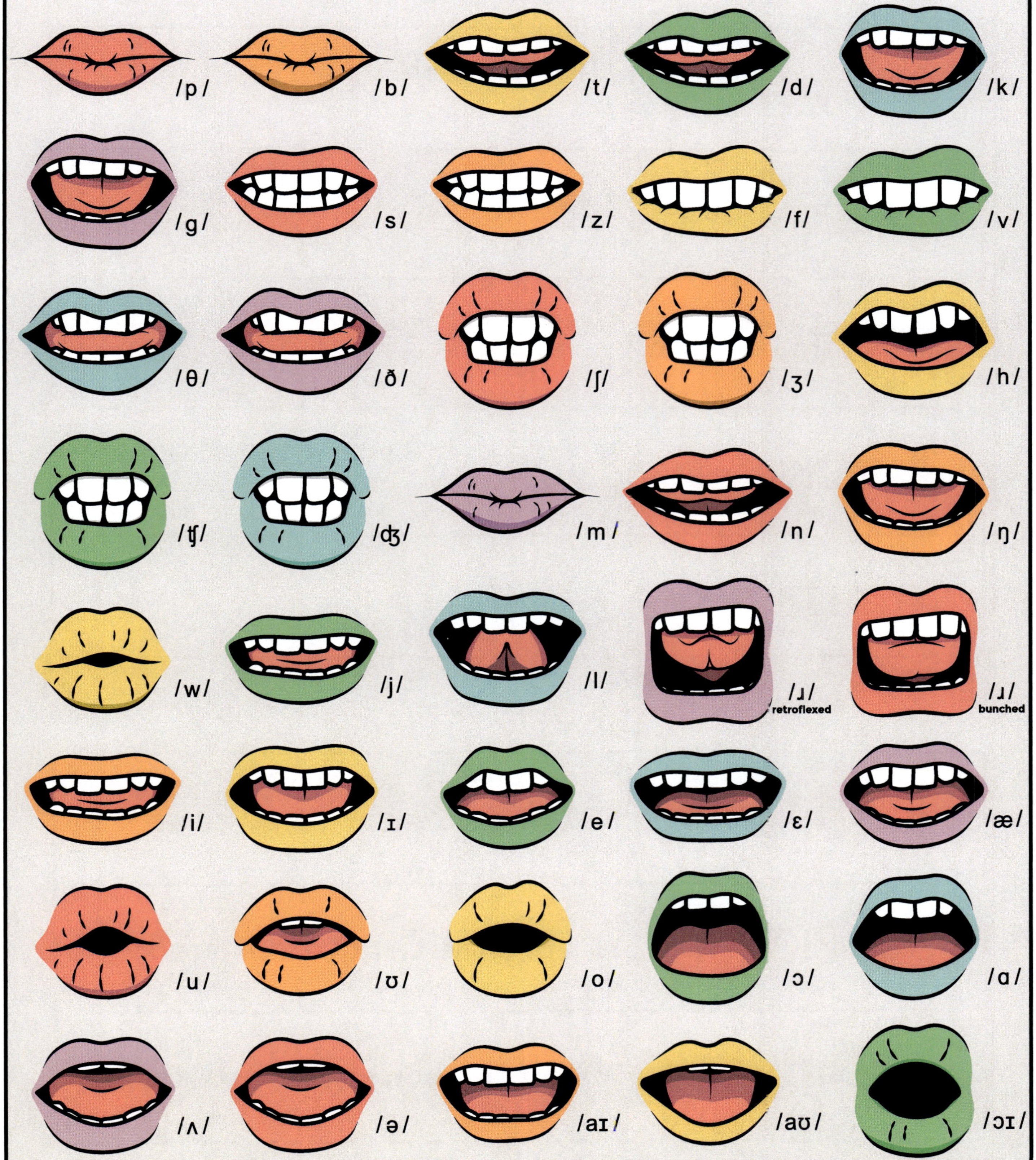

PEACHIE SPEECHIE'S

Speech Sound Handbook

Speech Sound Development

6 years	→	TH (voiceless) /θ/
5 years	→	TH (voiced) /ð/ ZH /ʒ/ r /ɹ/
4 years	→	V /v/ S /s/ Z /z/ SH /ʃ/ CH /ʧ/ J /ʤ/ L /l/
3 years	→	B /b/ T /t/ D /d/ K /k/ G /g/ M /m/ N /n/ NG /ŋ/ F /f/ H /h/ Y /j/ W /w/
2 years	→	P /p/

(Reference: Crowe & McLeod, 2020)

R Sound Aquisition

Age 2;11	→	50% of children have mastered R
Age 4;0	→	75% of children have mastered R
Age 5;7	→	90% of children have mastered R

(Reference: Crowe & McLeod, 2020)

PEACHIE SPEECHIE'S

Speech Sound Handbook

Speech Sound Checklist

Stimulability for Sounds in Isolation

Name: ______________________ **Age:** __________

Clinician: ______________________ **Date:** __________

6 years

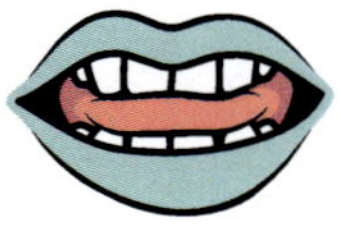
/θ/ ☐

5 years

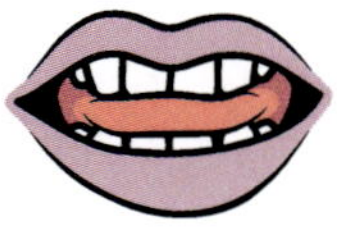
/ð/ ☐

/ʒ/ ☐

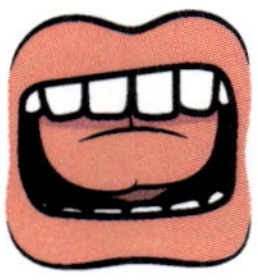
/ɹ/ ☐

4 years

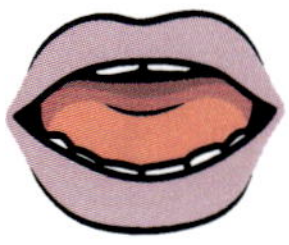
/ʌ/ ☐

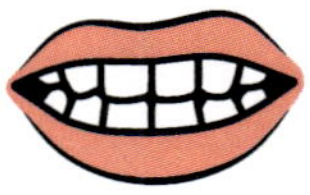
/s/ ☐

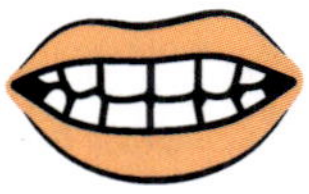
/z/ ☐

/ʃ/ ☐

/ʧ/ ☐

/ʤ/ ☐

/l/ ☐

3 years

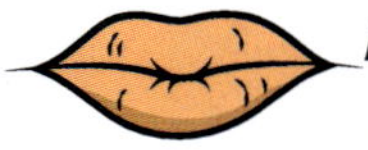
/b/ ☐

/t/ ☐

/d/ ☐

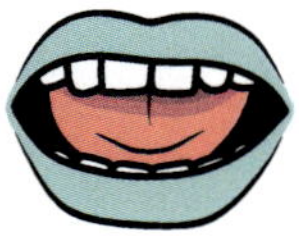
/k/ ☐

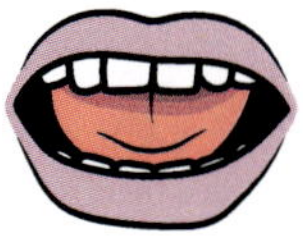
/g/ ☐

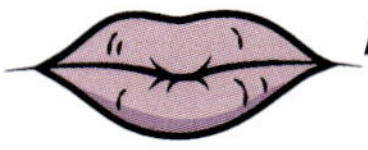
/m/ ☐

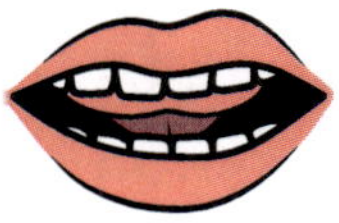
/n/ ☐

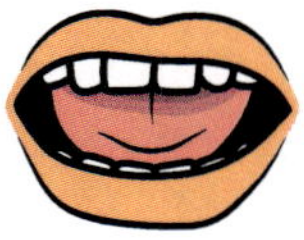
/ŋ/ ☐

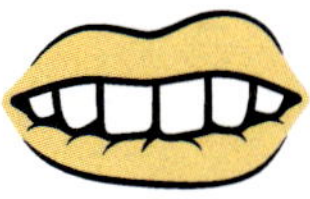
/f/ ☐

/h/ ☐

/w/ ☐

/j/ ☐

2 years

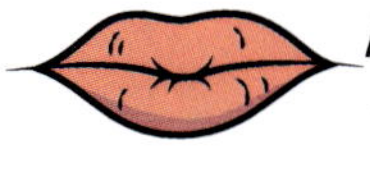
/p/ ☐

PEACHIE SPEECHIE'S

Speech Sound Handbook

Place Manner Voice Chart

			PLACE							
			LABIAL		CORONAL				DORSAL	
	MANNER	VOICING	BILABIAL	LABIODENTAL	DENTAL	ALVEOLAR	POSTALVEOLAR	PALATAL	VELAR	GLOTTAL
OBSTRUENTS	STOP	VOICELESS	p			t			k	ʔ
OBSTRUENTS	STOP	VOICED	b			d			g	
OBSTRUENTS	FRICATIVE	VOICELESS		f	θ	s	ʃ			h
OBSTRUENTS	FRICATIVE	VOICED		v	ð	z	ʒ			
OBSTRUENTS	AFFRICATE	VOICELESS					ʧ			
OBSTRUENTS	AFFRICATE	VOICED					ʤ			
SONORANTS	NASAL	VOICED	m			n			ŋ	
SONORANTS	LIQUID: LATERAL	VOICED				l				
SONORANTS	LIQUID: RHOTIC	VOICED					ɹ			
SONORANTS	GLIDE	VOICED	w					j	w	

PEACHIE SPEECHIE'S

Speech Sound Handbook

Vowel Quadrilateral

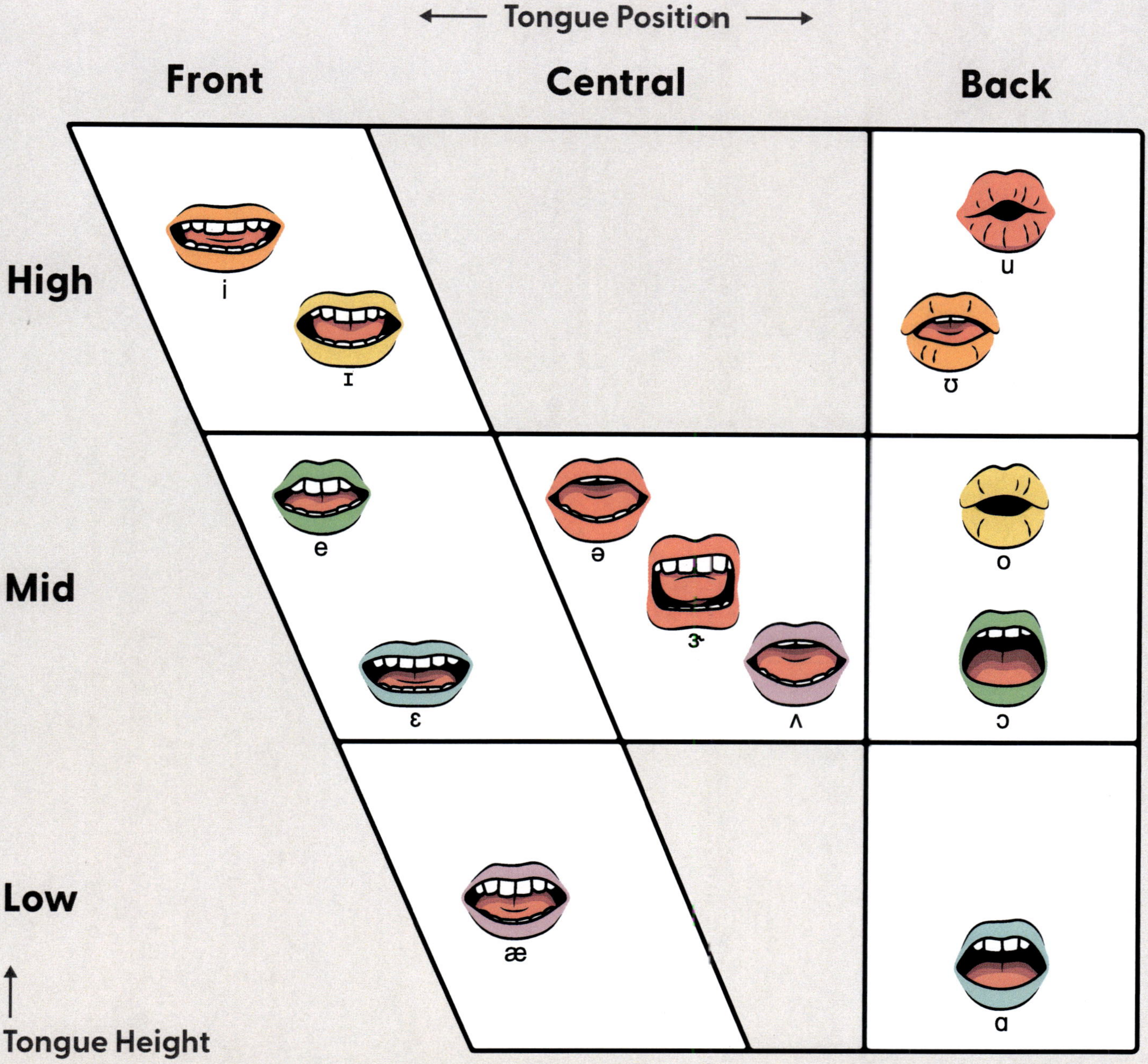

Speech Anatomy

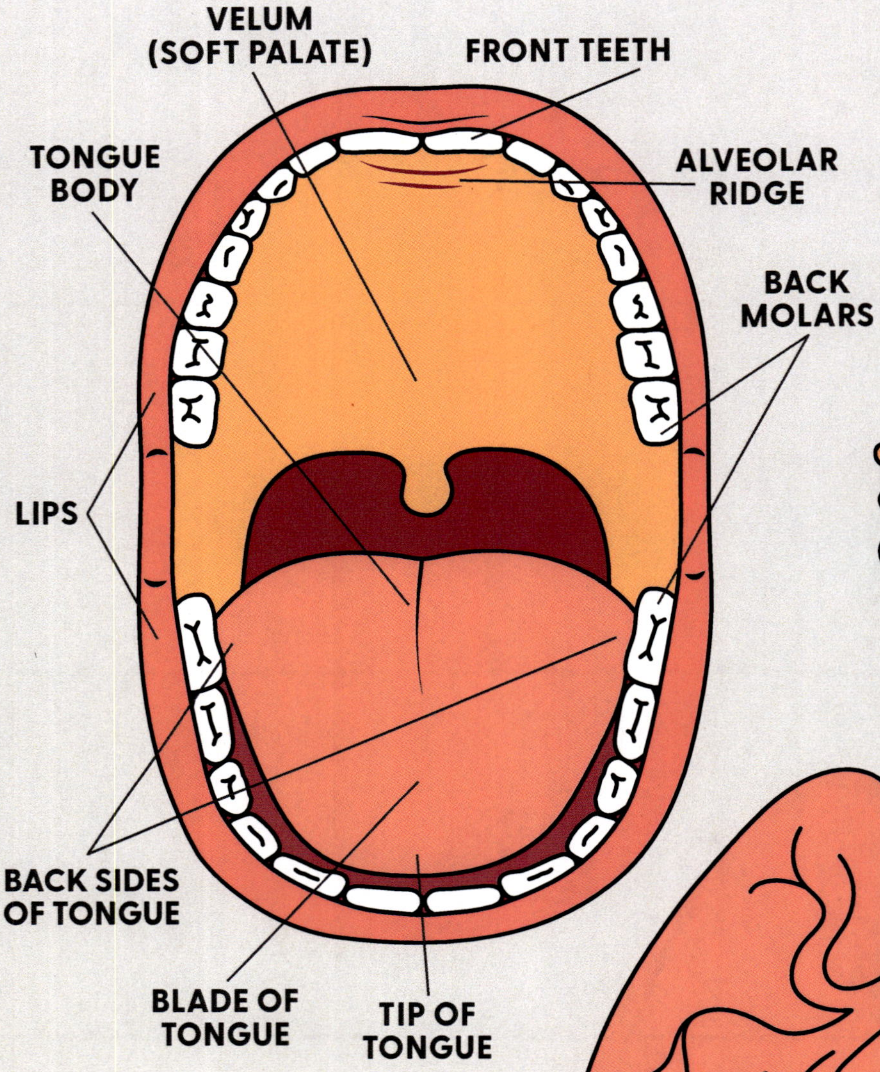

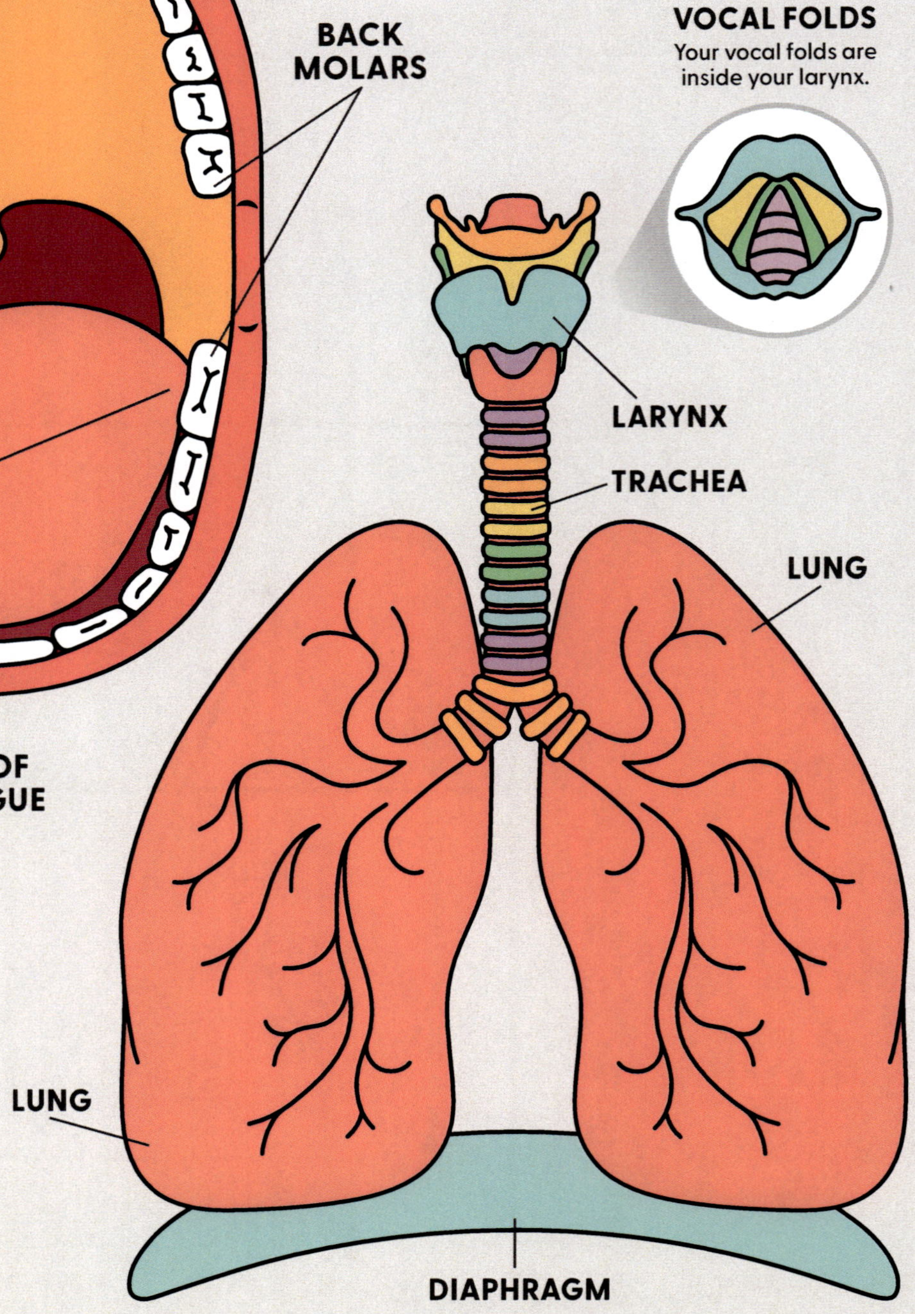

Traditional Articulation Therapy Strategies

Strategy	Description
Perceptual Training	The clinician teaches the child to identify the target sound and discriminate it from other sounds. For example, the clinician may present minimal pairs "red" and "wed" and ask the child which word contains the /ɹ/ sound. Or, the clinician may ask the child to raise their hand when they hear the target sound.
Modeling	Clinician models the sound and asks the child to repeat. The clinician may choose to exaggerate production, emphasizing the sound to draw attention to it. This is sometimes referred to as auditory stimulation.
Phonetic Placement Instructions	The clinician provides phonetic cues to teach the child how to make the sound. For example, the clinician might say, "Lift your tongue tip to your alveolar ridge" for the /l/ sound. Younger children may need simpler language such as, "Feel the bumps behind your teeth. Now, put the front of your tongue on those bumps". Other examples include telling the child, "turn your voice on" or "press your lips together".
Tactile Cues	The clinician uses motokinesthetic strategies to increase awareness of articulators and encourage accurate placement. Examples include rubbing a lollipop on the alveolar ridge to elicit tongue tip elevation or placing a hand on their neck to feel for voicing.
Visuals	The clinician can provide illustrated drawings, diagrams, plastic models, mirrors, hand symbols, etc. to teach the child how to say the sound. Examples include making a tongue out of play dough and lifting the tip to show movement for alveolar sounds or curling your fingertips back to represent the retroflex tongue shape for /ɹ/.
Shaping	The clinician starts with a sound already in the child's repertoire and uses successive approximations to shape that sound into the target sound. For example, starting with the /l/ sound and instructing the child to slide their tongue back along their palate to produce the retroflex /ɹ/.
Facilitating Contexts and Coarticulation	The clinician carefully selects words/sets of words to facilitate production. Certain contexts make it easier for some children to produce their target sound. This is referred to as a facilitating context. For example, it can be easier to produce an /s/ when it is immediately preceded by a /t/. Therefore, words like "cats" can facilitate an accurate /s/. Coarticulation refers to your mouth moving in anticipation of the next sound(s) in a word. For example, if a child can produce initial prevocalic /ɹ/ in words but is struggling to produce accurate final vocalic /aɹ/, you can pair the words Car→Red. The child anticipates the /ɹ/ in red and their tongue moves into place, assisting in production of accurate /aɹ/ in car.

(Reference: Bernthal, Bankston & Flipsen, 2009, VanRiper, 1990, Williams, McLeod, & McCauley 2021)

Articulation Supply List

Below you will find a list of my top 10 favorite items for articulation therapy. Many of these items are suggested throughout the book to assist with eliciting speech sounds. It is not absolutely necessary to have all of these things on hand, but I found them to be incredibly helpful during my time as a school-based SLP.

- Tongue depressors
- Dental swabs
- Play dough
- Mouth model
- Mirror
- Small lollipops
- Pen light
- Auditory feedback phone
- Circle shaped cereal (for the K and G sounds)
- Dental flossers (for the R sound)

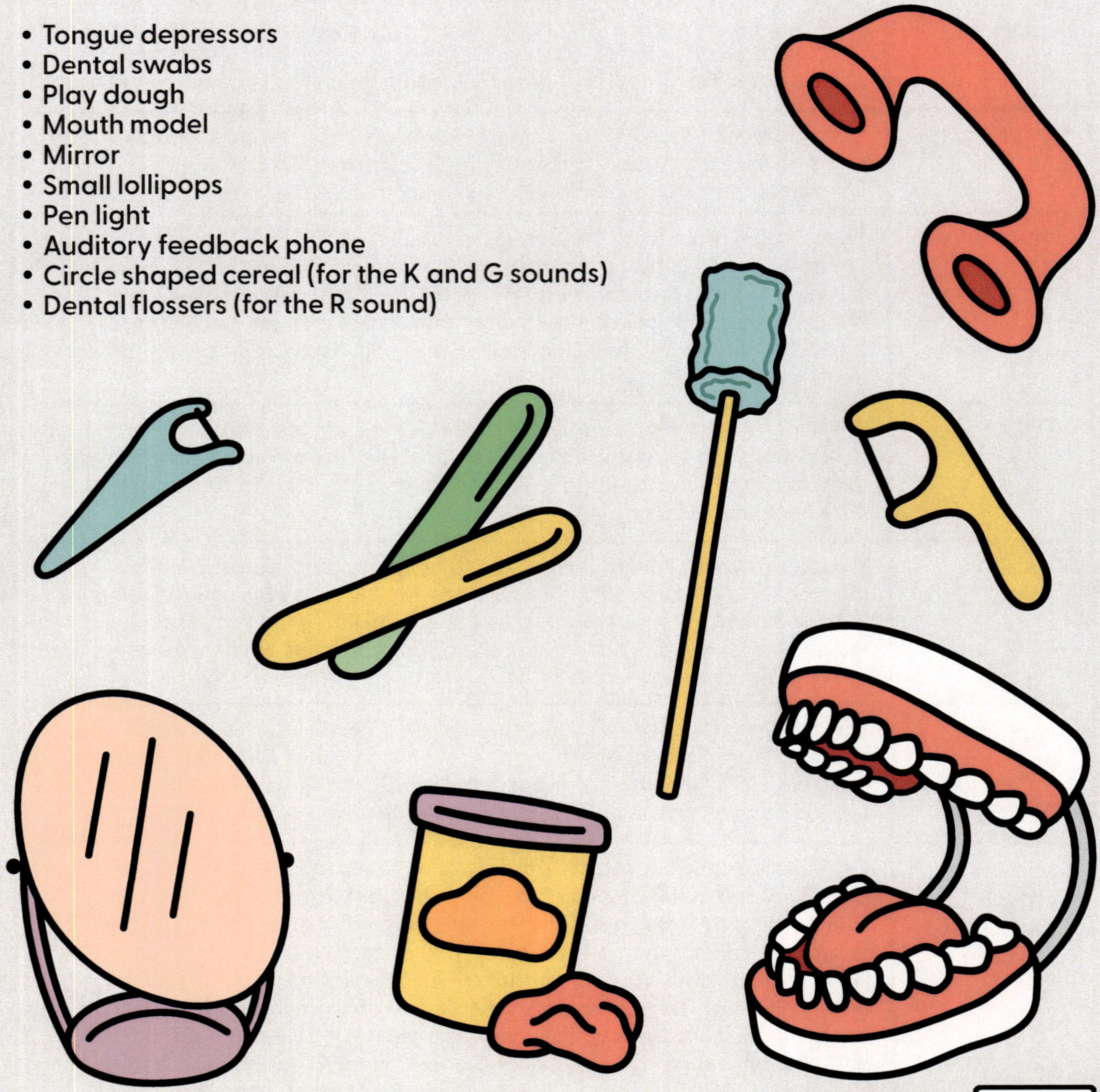

Scan this QR code to read about different mouth models

SCAN ME

Peachie Speechie's Tongue Dough Recipe

I love making my own play dough to use during speech therapy sessions, and I call it TONGUE DOUGH! This tongue dough is easy to make, smells great, and looks a lot like a real tongue.

Ingredients:

- 1 cup all purpose white flour
- 1/2 cup salt
- 2 tsp. cream of tartar
- 2 packets of unsweetened KoolAid (red/cherry)
- 1 cup water
- 1 tablespoon clear baby oil*
  ** If you think your students might eat the dough, use vegetable oil instead of baby oil.*

Directions:

- Mix dry ingredients in a bowl.
- Put baby oil and water in a pot on the stove and turn heat on medium-low.
- Add dry ingredients to the water on the stove and stir.
- Keep stirring until a dough ball forms.
- As soon as a dough ball forms, take the pot off the heat and keep mixing. You may want to fold it with a spatula at this point.
- Let cool for a few minutes. Once it is cool enough to handle, squish and knead it with your hands to get out any little bumps. Keep kneading until it's nice and smooth.

Here's an example

Note: You can use different colors of KoolAid to change the color of the dough.

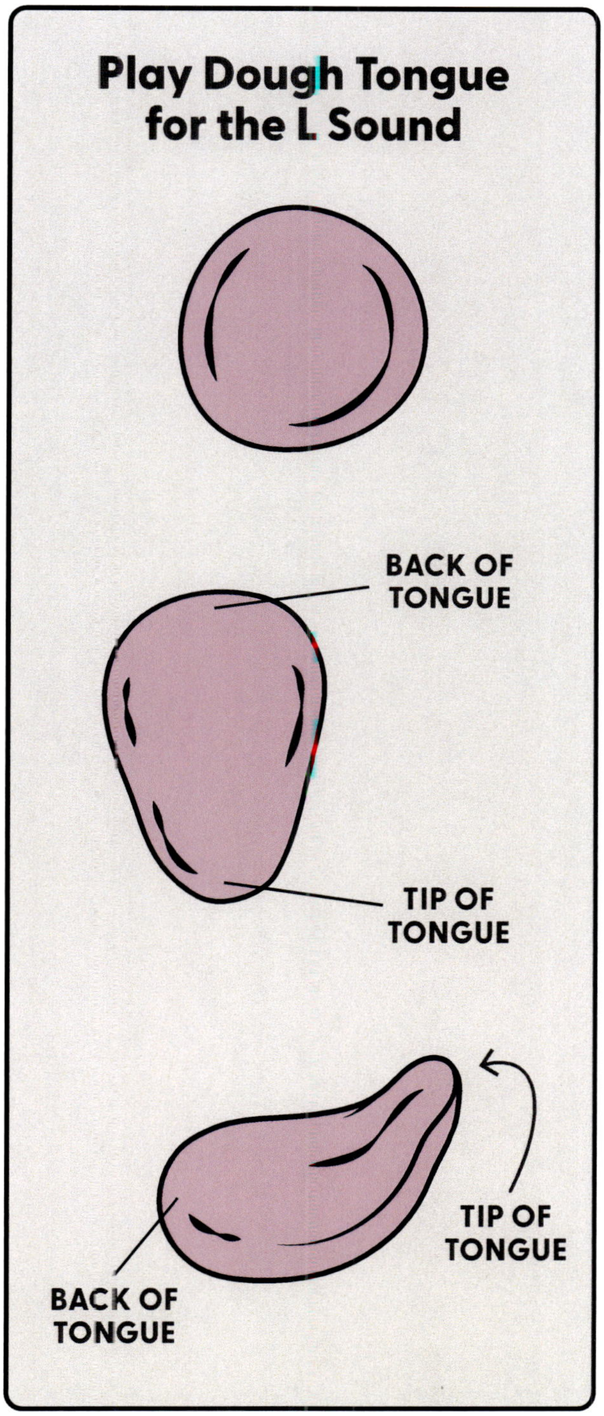

Consonants

The P Sound

/p/

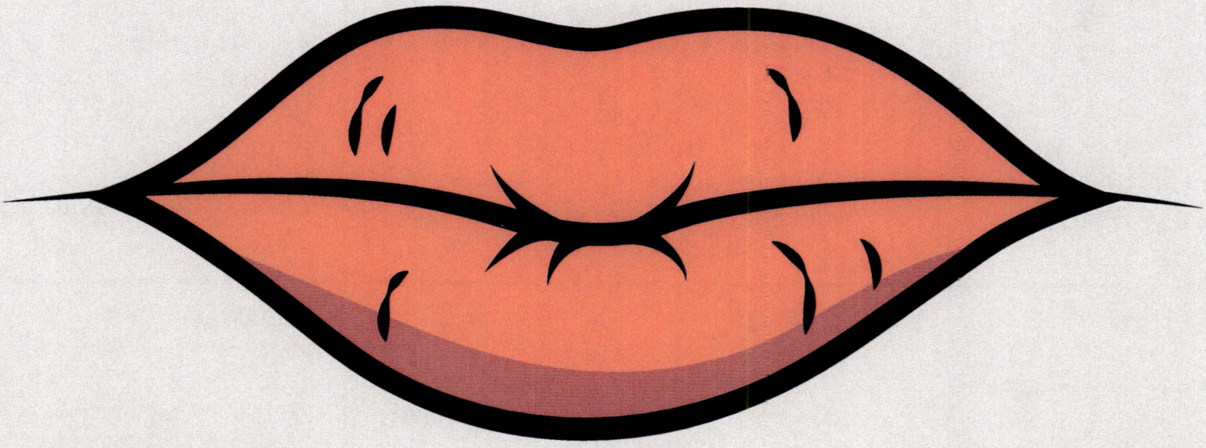

How to Say the P Sound

- Put your lips together.
- Puff out air.
- Keep your voice off.

PEACHIE SPEECHIE'S

Speech Sound Handbook

/p/ Word List

Initial

1 Syllable

Pace
Pack
Page
Paid
Paint
Pair
Pal
Pale
Palm
Pam
Pant
Park
Part
Pass
Pat
Path
Pause
Paw
Pay
Pea
Peace
Peach
Pear
Peek
Pen
Pet
Pick
Pie
Pig
Pill
Pin
Pinch
Pine
Pink
Point
Poke
Poll
Pond
Pool
Poor
Pork
Pound
Pours
Puff
Pull
Punch
Purse
Push
Put

2 Syllables

Package
Packet
Painted
Pancake
Panic
Parfait
Parking
Parrot
Passing
Pastry
Pattern
Peanut
Pebble
Pecan
Pedal
Pencil
Penny
Perfect
Perform
Pickle
Picnic
Picture
Pigeon
Pillow
Pinwheel
Pirate
Pizza
Pocket
Poem
Police
Pollen
Pony
Postal
Power
Pudding
Puddle
Puffin
Punish
Puzzle
Python

3 Syllables

Pacific
Pajamas
Panama
Parachute
Paradise
Paragraph
Parallel
Passenger
Patriot
Penalty
Perfection
Performance
Period
Personal
Petunia
Piano
Piggybank
Pioneer
Politics
Positive
Potato
Pottery
Pyramid

Medial

Apart
Apple
Chipper
Copy
Coupon
Deeper
Diaper
Happy
Hippo
Hopping
Keeping
Leopard
Napkin
Napping
Open
Oppose
Rapid
Repair
Report
Shipping
Sleeping
Soapy
Stopping
Super
Teapot
Toothpaste
Upon
Whopper
Wrapper
Zipper

Final

Ape
Beep
Cap
Cape
Cheep
Chip
Creep
Cup
Dip
Drip
Flip
Flop
Gap
Group
Hop
Hoop
Jeep
Jump
Keep
Lamp
Lap
Leap
Lip
Loop
Map
Mop
Nap
Rip
Rope
Shape
Sheep
Ship
Sip
Skip
Snap
Soap
Stripe
Stop
Soup
Sweep
Tap
Top
Trap
Type
Up
Weep
Wrap
Yap
Zap
Zip

Challenge

Multiple positions within the word

Ping Pong
Pimple
Papa
Pepper
Poppy
Pumpkin
Peep
Pop
Pipe
Poop
Puppy
Puppet
Popcorn
Paper
Purple
People
Pineapple
Peppermint
Papaya

Eliciting /p/

P is a voiceless, bilabial, stop sound. The lips come together and then air pressure builds and releases into the sound. Children have typically mastered this sound by age 2.

Eliciting P

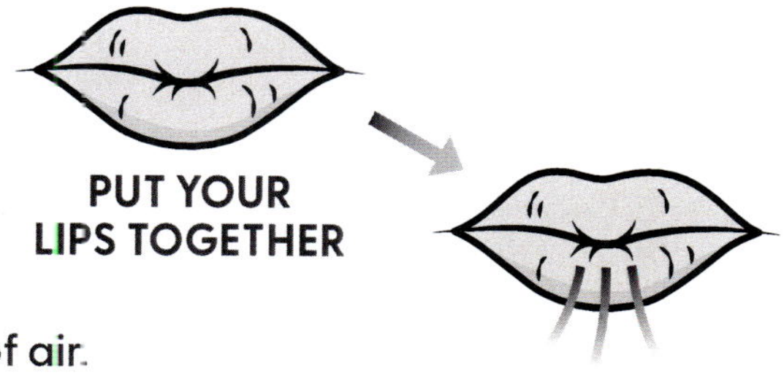

- Demonstrate lip closure by using your fingers to gently close their lips.
- Give step-by-step placement instructions.
  1. Close your lips.
  2. Release a puff of air.
- Have the child hold their hand in front of your mouth as you produce /p/ so they can feel the puff of air.
- Hold a small hand mirror up to your mouth so they can see the condensation from releasing the air.
- Press your thumb and index finger together near your mouth as a cue for lip closure as you model the sound.
- Have the child close their lips around a thin piece of rolled out fruit leather and press to demonstrate lip closure, holding it in place. Then, remove the fruit leather and have them practice producing the /p/ sound. This can also be done with a tongue depressor or thin coffee straw.
- Rub a lollipop along the upper and lower lips where they meet and tell the child to stick the lips together and then release the quiet puff of air. You could also use a dental swab or gloved finger instead of a lollipop to draw attention to the lips.
- Popping Bubbles: Ask the child to "make a bubble" by puffing up their cheeks with air and then "pop the bubble" by releasing the air into the /p/ sound. Once they can do this, work on making the sound without puffing out the cheeks.
- Hopping into the P Sound: Have the child say /ha/ and then close their lips to stop the air. Then, ask them to release the air, resulting in the word "hop". You can do it continuously, so it sounds like /hapapapa/ with aspiration on the /p/ sounds.
- Song to help remember /p/ placement. Lyrics: Lips together for the P. Lips together for the P. Then release a puff of air. Sounds so good to me! Scan the QR code for the video of this song.

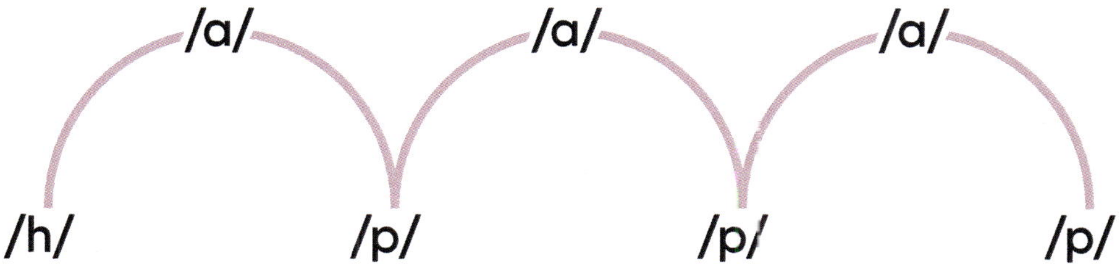

Scan this QR code to go directly to our free video

SCAN ME

The B Sound

/b/

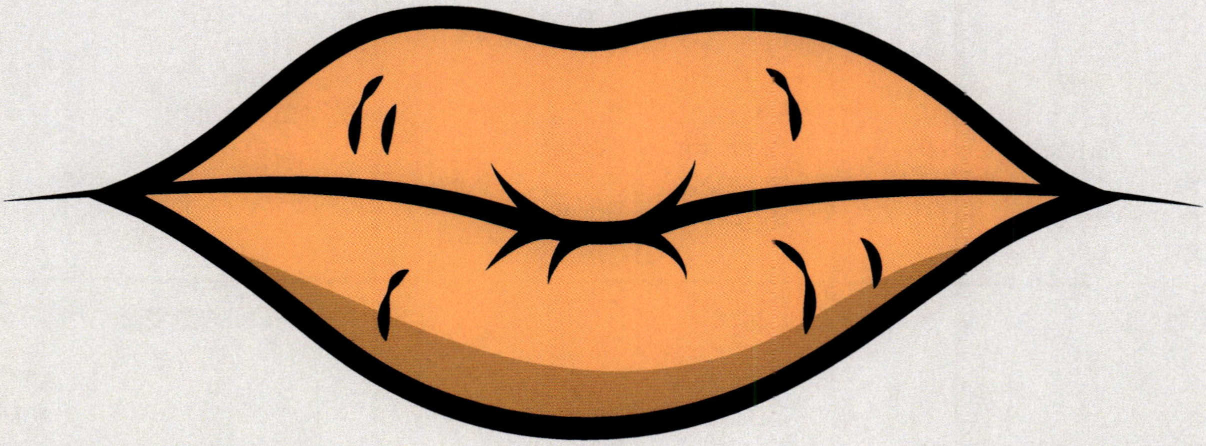

How to Say the B Sound

- Put your lips together.
- Puff out air.
- Turn your voice on.

PEACHIE SPEECHIE'S

Speech Sound Handbook

/b/ Word List

Initial

1 Syllable

Baa	Bear	Book
Back	Bed	Boom
Bag	Bee	Boss
Bake	Beef	Both
Ball	Beep	Bow
Bang	Beg	Bowl
Bank	Bell	Box
Bare	Belt	Boy
Bark	Bench	Bug
Barn	Best	Bump
Base	Bike	Bunch
Bat	Bill	Bun
Bath	Bird	Burp
Be	Birth	Bus
Beach	Bite	Bush
Bead	Boat	But
Beak	Bone	Buzz
Bean	Boo	Bye

2 Syllables

Backup	Began	Button
Bacon	Behave	Busy
Badger	Believe	Butter
Bagel	Berry	Buzzer
Ballet	Biking	
Balloon	Biscuit	
Banner	Boa	
Barrel	Body	
Basement	Bonus	
Basket	Booster	
Baton	Bossy	
Beagle	Bottle	
Beaver	Bucket	
Because	Buddy	
Become	Bully	
Bedroom	Bunny	
Before	Buried	

3 Syllables

- Bakery
- Balcony
- Baltimore
- Banana
- Bandana
- Battery
- Beginner
- Behavior
- Bicycle
- Bodyguard
- Bologna
- Buffalo
- Bulletin
- Buttercup
- Butterfly

Medial

About	Ladybug
Above	Mailbox
Aerobics	Maybe
Cabin	Neighbor
Cabinet	Obey
Cable	Oboe
Cheeseburger	October
Cowboy	Rabbit
Elbow	Ribbon
Goodbye	Robot
Habit	Rubber
Hobby	Ruby
Honeybee	Subject
Kickball	Teabag
Labor	Tugboat
Label	Volleyball

Final

Cab	Slob
Cob	Sob
Crab	Sub
Cub	Swab
Cube	Tab
Dab	Tribe
Grab	Tub
Job	Tube
Knob	Web
Lab	
Lobe	
Mob	
Rib	
Robe	
Scab	
Scrub	

Challenge

Multiple positions within the word

Babe	Blueberry
Barbara	Cobweb
Blackberry	Bathrobe
Babble	
Baboon	
Bamboo	
Barbie	
Bobcat	
Bib	
Baby	
Bubble	
Baseball	
Basketball	
Bobcat	
Bye-Bye	

PEACHIE SPEECHIE'S

Speech Sound Handbook

Eliciting /b/

B is a voiced, bilabial, stop sound. The lips come together and then air pressure builds and releases into the voiced sound. Children have typically mastered this sound by age 3.

Eliciting B

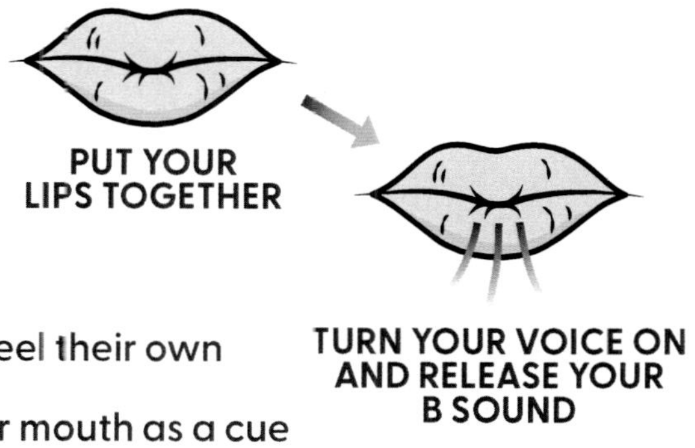

- Demonstrate lip closure by using your fingers to gently close their lips.
- Give step-by-step placement instructions.
    1. Close your lips.
    2. Release a puff of air with your voice turned on.
- Demonstrate voicing by allowing the child to touch your throat as you say the /b/ sound. They can also feel their own throat as they practice.
- Press your thumb and index finger together near your mouth as a cue for lip closure as you model the sound.
- Have the child close their lips around a thin rolled out piece of fruit leather and press to demonstrate lip closure, holding it in place. Then, remove the fruit leather and have them practice producing the /b/ sound. This can also be done with a tongue depressor or thin coffee straw.
- Rub a lollipop along the upper and lower lips where they meet and tell the child to stick the lips together and then release the sound with their voice on. You could also use a dental swab or gloved finger instead of a lollipop to draw attention to the lips.
- Boo-Boo Ghost Sound: Shape from /u/ by having them sustain the /u/ sound ("ooo") and then closing their lips together and then releasing them to make the /b/ sound ("ooo-boo"). If they need further assistance with lip closure, you can have them sustain /u/ and then use your fingers to gently, repeatedly close their lips. This will sound like "ooo-boo-boo-boo-boo".

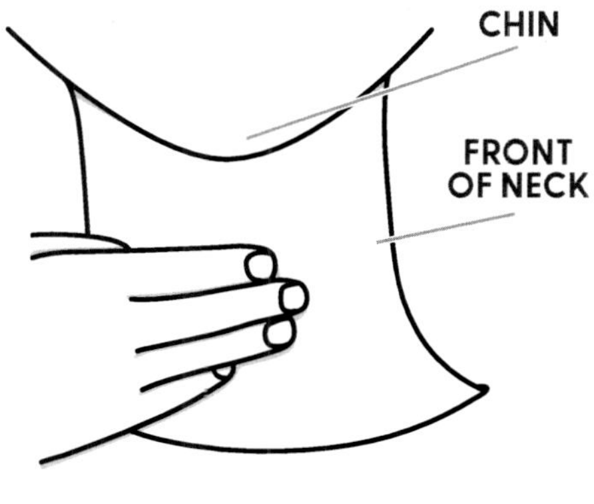

- Baa-Baa Sheep Sound: Start by having them say /a/ and then prompt them to close their jaw while continuing say /a/. Then, have them quickly close and open their lips. This will sound like "ahh-baa". If they need further assistance with lip closure, you can have them sustain /ah/ and then use your fingers to gently, repeatedly close their lips. This will sound like "ahh-baa-baa". You can also shape from /ʌ/ using this method.
- Song to help remember the /b/ placement. Lyrics: Lips together, voice turns on, voice turns on, voice turns on. Lips together, voice turns on. Let's say the B sound! Scan the QR code for the video of this song.

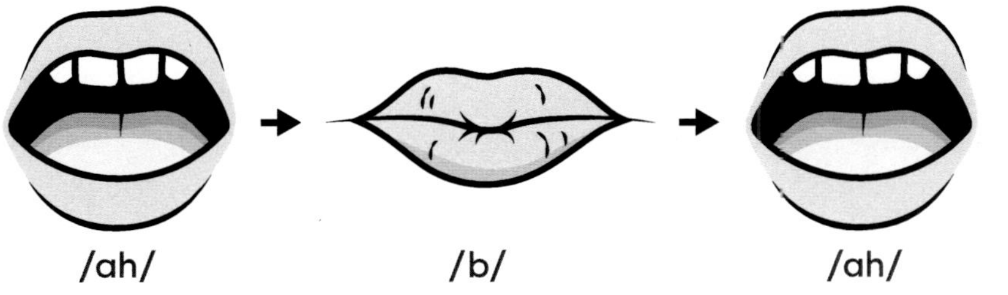

Scan this QR code to go directly to our free video

SCAN ME

The T Sound

/t/

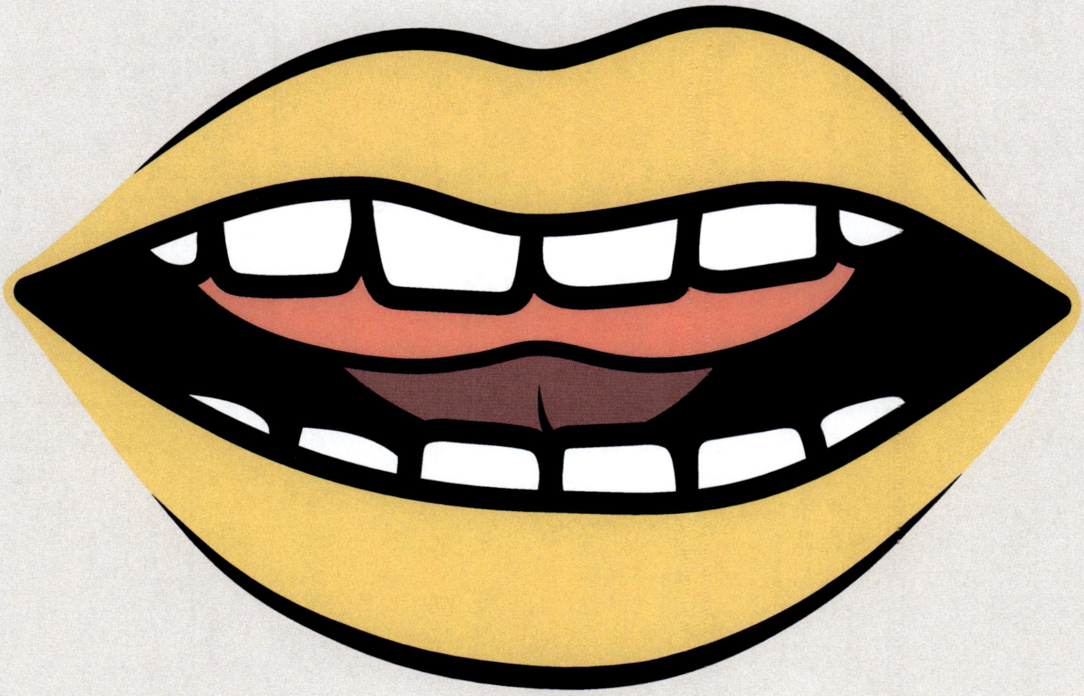

How to Say the T Sound

- Put your tongue tip up to your alveolar ridge.
- Release a burst of air.
- Keep your voice off.

PEACHIE SPEECHIE'S

Speech Sound Handbook

/t/ Word List

Initial

1 Syllable

Tab
Tail
Take
Talk
Tan
Tank
Tap
Tape
Task
Tea
Team
Tears
Tease
Tee
Teen
Teeth
Tell
Ten
Tense
Tie
Time
Tip
Tire
To
Toad
Toe
Tongue
Took
Tool
Tooth
To
Tore
Toss
Touch
Town
Toy
Tub
Tube
Tunes
Turn
Try
Type

2 Syllables

Tabby
Table
Taco
Taffy
Taking
Talent
Tangle
Tanning
Tapping
Tardy
Tassel
Taxi
Teacher
Teacup
Teddy
Teenage
Tennis
Texas
Tiger
Tiny
Tired
Tissue
Today
Token
Tonsil
Topic
Towel
Tuesday
Tulip
Tuna
Turkey
Turnip

3 Syllables

Tablecloth
Taekwondo
Takeover
Tamale
Taxicab
Teachable
Technical
Teenager
Telephone
Terrible
Terrific
Together
Tomorrow
Tornado
Tuition
Typical

Medial

Attend
Attic
Baton
Beauty
Butter
Button
Cheetah
City
Cottage
Cotton
Cutting
Dating
Eaten
Eighty
Fatigue
Fighter
Floating
Getting
Guitar
Hotel
Kitty
Later
Letter
Litter
Lotto
Matter
Mitten
Motel
Naughty
Ninety
Otter
Pattern
Photo
Pouting
Pretty
Rattle
Rotten
Saturday
Saturn
Setting
Sit-up
Sweater
Sweeter
Voting
Water

Final

At
Ate
Bat
Bite
Boat
Boot
Bought
But
Cat
Caught
Chat
Cheat
Coat
Cut
Cute
Eat
Fat
Feet
Fight
Fruit
Get
Goat
Got
Hat
Heat
Hot
It
Jet
Kite
Knot
Late
Light
Mat
Meet
Might
Mute
Net
Not
Note
Nut
Oat
Out
Plate
Put
Quit
Rat
Sat
Seat
Set
Shut
Sit
Skate
Spot
Sweet
That
Throat
Vote
Wait
Wet
What
White
Wrote
Yet

Challenge

Multiple positions within the word

Tablet
Treat
Tote
Toot
Tattoo
Turtle
Toaster
Tattle
Ticket
Title
Talented
Talkative
Toothpaste
Tournament
Territory
Potato
Tomato
Taught
Tight
Teapot
Toilet
Tonight
Tortilla

Some medial /t/ words are pronounced with a "flap T", which is written as /ɾ/ in IPA and sounds similar to quick light /d/.

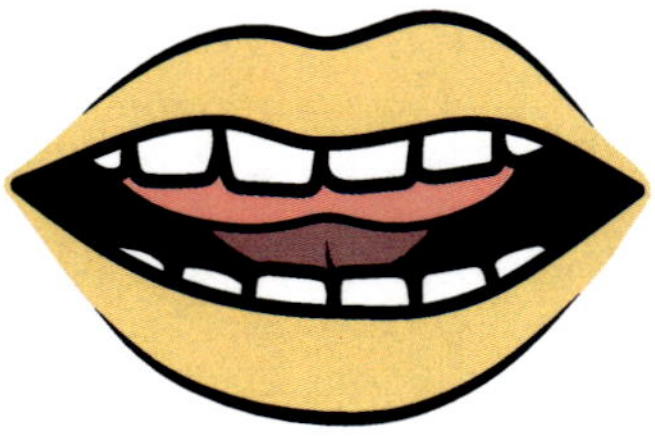

Eliciting /t/

T is a voiceless, lingua alveolar, stop sound. The tongue tip lifts to touch the alveolar ridge. The sides of the tongue are also lifted, touching the top molars. Breath pressure builds and is released as the tongue tip is pulled away from the alveolar ridge. This burst of air makes the T sound. Children have typically mastered this sound by age 3.

Eliciting T

- Point out the alveolar ridge and tongue tip on a mouth model or illustration. Have them feel the bumps of the alveolar ridge on the mouth model and their own mouth to get familiar with anatomy involved in production of the /t/ sound.
- Give step-by-step placement instructions.
    1. **Lift your tongue tip to your alveolar ridge.**
    2. **Release a burst of air.**
- If they are having difficulty understanding the "burst of air", simply tell them to lift their tongue up to the alveolar ridge and blow air out while dropping their tongue down. You can also compare it to the burst of air required for /p/.
- Explain that some air pressure will build behind their tongue as it is lifted to the alveolar ridge. The tongue drops a bit as this pressure is released and that makes the burst. You can demonstrate this with a mouth model and plastic tongue. Scan the QR code for a video demonstration.
- Use your hands to show tongue movement. Hold one hand out, palm down, representing the roof of your mouth and alveolar ridge. Bring the other hand palm up to meet it, representing your tongue. Quickly tap and drop your fingertips ("tongue tip") to demonstrate the quick release of the tongue tip from the alveolar ridge.
- Rub the alveolar ridge with a lollipop, dental swab, or gloved finger to increase awareness of it. Ask the child to bring their tongue tip to the place you just touched and then release the burst of air for /t/.
- Place a small dot of peanut butter or marshmallow fluff on the alveolar ridge to encourage tongue tip elevation.
- Point above your upper lip as you model the sound to remind the child to lift the tongue tip up to the alveolar ridge.
- Rename the /t/ sound. Call it the clock sound (tick-tock sound) as you practice.
- Shape from the /s/ sound. Have the child sustain the /s/ and then lift their tongue tip up to press against the alveolar ridge and stop the air mid-stream. Then, have them forcefully release the quiet burst of air into the aspirated /t/ sound.
- Shape from the /ʧ/ sound. Tell the child to make the /ʧ/ sound while smiling wide and making their tongue tip pointy.
- Song to help remember the /t/ placement. Lyrics: Put your tongue up for T right here /t/-/t/. Then let out a little bit of air /t/-/t/. Put your tongue tip up for T, Oh it sounds so good to me, Put your tongue up for T right here /t/-/t/! Scan the QR code for the video of this song.

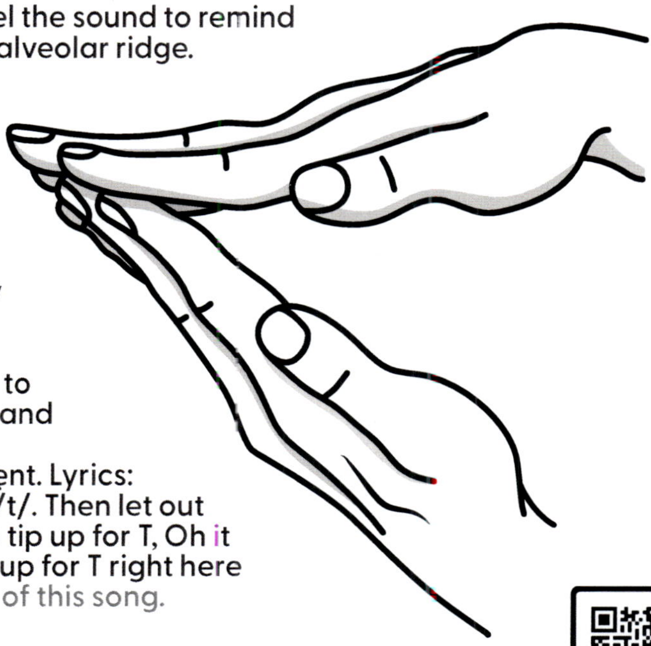

Scan this QR code to go directly to our free video

SCAN ME

The D Sound

/d/

How to Say the D Sound

- Put your tongue tip up to your alveolar ridge.
- Release a burst of air.
- Turn your voice on.

PEACHIE SPEECHIE'S

Speech Sound Handbook

/d/ Word List

Initial

1 Syllable

Dye, Do, Day, Date, Done, Duck, Door, Don't, Dove, Down, Dance, Dash, Dark, Deep, Dear, Desk, Dent, Deck, Dip, Dish, Dig, Dive, Dice, Dial, Dog, Doll, Dot, Dime, Dine, Dress, Drop, Dry

2 Syllables

Daily, Daisy, Dancer, Danger, Daughter, Daycare, Deacon, Debate, Decor, Delay, Delete, Denim, Dentist, Desert, Design, Device, Dial, Dinner, Dimple, Dizzy, Doctor, Doing, Dollar, Dolphin, Donate, Donkey, Donut, Doorway, Dozen, During, Duty

3 Syllables

Dangerous, Decimal, Decision, Decorate, Delaware, Delicate, Develop, Diagram, Dialect, Diary, Difficult, Dimension, Dinosaur, Diploma, Direction, Dishtowel, Distribute, Division, Document, Duplicate, Dynamite

Medial

Adding, Birthday, Body, Calendar, Cider, Edit, Headache, Hidden, Idea, Ladder, Lady, Leader, Louder, Meadow, Medicine, Muddy, Nobody, Nodding, Radio, Reading, Ready, Riding, Shadow, Soda, Spider, Sudden, Today, Under, Video, Wedding, Woody

Final

Add, Afraid, Allowed, Bad, Bead, Bed, Bread, Cloud, Could, Cried, Food, Gifted, Glad, Good, Grade, Had, Head, Hide, Hood, Kid, Lead, Lid, Lied, Loud, Mad, Made, Mood, Mud, Need, Odd, Old, Paid, Played, Pointed, Pride, Read, Red, Ride, Sad, Said, Salad, Sand, Send, Should, Side, Toad, Trade, Upload, Used, We'd, Would, You'd

Challenge

Multiple positions within the word

Dud, Dude, Decade, Download, Dad, Did, Demanding, Divided, Decided, Died

Eliciting /d/

D is a voiced, lingua alveolar, stop sound. The tongue tip lifts to touch the alveolar ridge. The sides of the tongue are also lifted, touching the top molars. Breath pressure builds and is released as the tongue tip is pulled away from the alveolar ridge. This slight burst of air with the voice turned on makes the D sound. Children have typically mastered this sound by age 3.

Eliciting D

- Point out the alveolar ridge and tongue tip on a mouth model or illustration. Have them feel the bumps of the alveolar ridge on the mouth model and their own mouth to get familiar with anatomy involved in production of the /d/ sound.
- Distinguish the /d/ from the /t/ sound by having the child place their hand on clinician's throat during production of both /d/ and /t/. You might want to call it "Loud T Sound" if they already know how to produce an accurate /t/.
- Give step-by-step placement instructions.
    1. Lift your tongue tip to your alveolar ridge.
    2. Release a burst of air with your voice turned on.
- Explain that some air pressure will build behind their tongue as it is lifted to the alveolar ridge. The tongue drops a bit as this pressure is released as the voice turns on for /d/. You can demonstrate this with a mouth model and plastic tongue. Scan the QR code for a video demonstration.
- Use your hands to show tongue movement. Hold one hand out, palm down, representing the roof of your mouth and alveolar ridge. Bring the other hand palm up to meet it, representing your tongue. Quickly tap and drop your fingertips ("tongue tip") to demonstrate the quick release of the tongue tip from the alveolar ridge. See illustration of this in the /t/ section of this book.

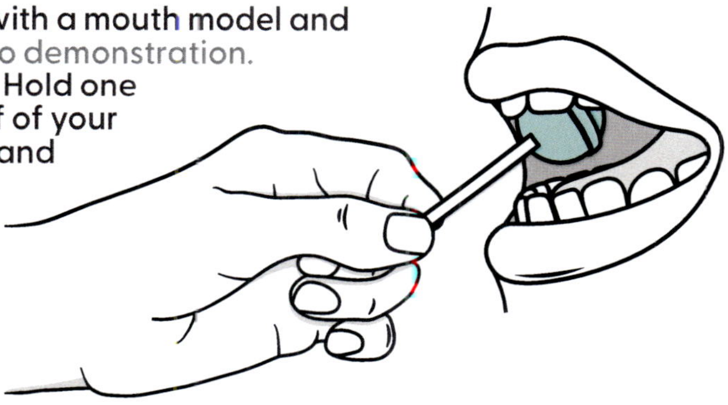

- Rub the alveolar ridge with a lollipop, dental swab, or gloved finger to increase awareness of it. Ask the child to bring their tongue tip to the place you just touched and then release sound for /d/.
- Place a small dot of peanut butter or marshmallow fluff on the alveolar ridge to encourage tongue tip elevation.
- Point above your upper lip and place your hand on your throat as you model the sound to remind the child to lift the tongue tip up to the alveolar ridge and turn their voice on.
- Shape from the /i/ sound ("eee"). Have the child sustain the /i/ sound and then quickly press their tongue tip up to the alveolar ridge in a tapping motion. This may sound like "Ee-Dee-Dee-Dee".
- Song to help remember the /d/ placement. Lyrics: Tongue goes up to say the D, Voice turns on, Practice with me /d/! Scan the QR code for the video of this song.

Scan this QR code to go directly to our free video

SCAN ME

The K Sound

/k/

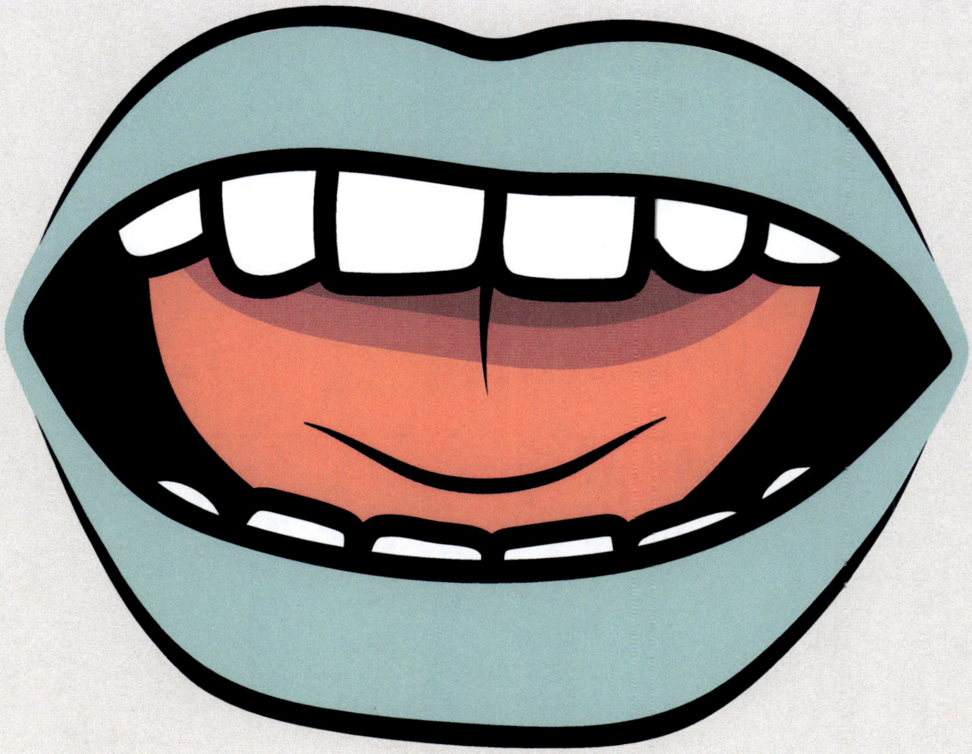

How to Say the K Sound

- Lift the back of your tongue to your soft palate and release a burst of air.
- Keep your voice off.

PEACHIE SPEECHIE'S

Speech Sound Handbook

/k/ Word List

Initial

1 Syllable

Cab
Cage
Call
Came
Camp
Can
Can't
Cap
Cape
Car
Care
Cart
Case
Cast
Cat
Caught
Coach
Coat
Coin
Cold
Come
Cone
Cool
Cop
Cord
Cost
Couch
Could
Count
Cow
Cup
Cut
Keep
Key
Kid
Kind
King
Kiss
Kite

2 Syllables

Cabin
Cable
Camel
Camper
Campus
Candy
Cannot
Canvas
Careful
Carpet
Carrot
Cartoon
Carry
Castle
Coffee
Color
Comma
Comment
Complete
Concert
Copy
Cousin
Cover
Cozy
Cushion
Kansas
Kelly
Kickball
Kindness
Kissing
Kitchen

3 Syllables

Calendar
Canada
Canary
Cantaloupe
Capital
Caribou
Carousel
Casserole
Casual
Coloring
Comedy
Computer
Continue
Consider
Covering
Customer
Kangaroo
Karate
Kentucky
Koala

Medial

Acorn
Bacon
Baking
Because
Biking
Bucket
Broccoli
Chicken
Circus
Donkey
Echo
Focus
Hiccup
Jacket
Lucky
Monkey
Napkin
Package
Pelican
Pocket
Raccoon
Racket
Rocket
Shaking
Sneaker
Soccer
Taco
Taken
Talking
Vacation
Vocal
Weekend

Final

Ache
Attack
Back
Basic
Bike
Book
Break
Cheek
Duck
Fake
Hack
Hike
Joke
Lake
Like
Look
Luck
Magic
Make
Neck
Notebook
Oak
Pack
Panic
Pick
Rake
Rack
Shook
Sick
Smoke
Snack
Snake
Sock
Speak
Stack
Stick
Stomach
Talk
Took
Truck
Wake
Walk
Yolk

Challenge

Multiple positions within the word

Comic
Cooking
Tick-Tok
Cake
Cactus
Cookbook
Cookie
Correct
Cracker
Picnic
Pancake
Coconut
Kentucky
Cucumber
Tic-Tac-Toe
Cupcake
Click
Cook
Kick

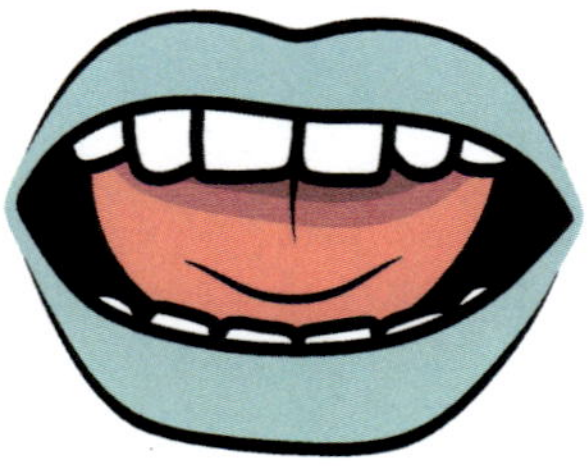

Eliciting /k/

K is a voiceless velar stop sound. The back of the tongue (dorsum) lifts to touch the velum. Then, the back of the tongue quickly drops from the velum, releasing a burst of air. Children have typically mastered this sound by age 3.

Eliciting K

- Use a mouth model and/or illustrations to point out the velum and back of tongue to make the child aware of key articulators.
- Have the child stick their tongue out in the mirror and use a tongue depressor to point out the tip of the tongue vs. the back of the tongue. Explain that the K sound needs the back of the tongue to elevate.
- Give step-by-step placement instructions.
    1. **Lift the back of your tongue to your soft palate.**
    2. **Release a burst of quiet air.**
- Make a tongue out of play dough and have the child lift the back of the tongue up to represent the movement required for /k/.
- Use your thumb to touch and gently press up under the chin as they practice saying /k/.
- Use your hand to show tongue shape with the back of the hand ("tongue") elevated. Hold your hand by your throat as you model the sound.
- Gently touch the child's velum and back of tongue with a lollipop or dental swab to increase awareness of articulators.
- Use a lollipop to gently push back the tongue in the mouth, and hold the tongue tip down as they practice saying /k/. This can also be done with a tongue depressor.

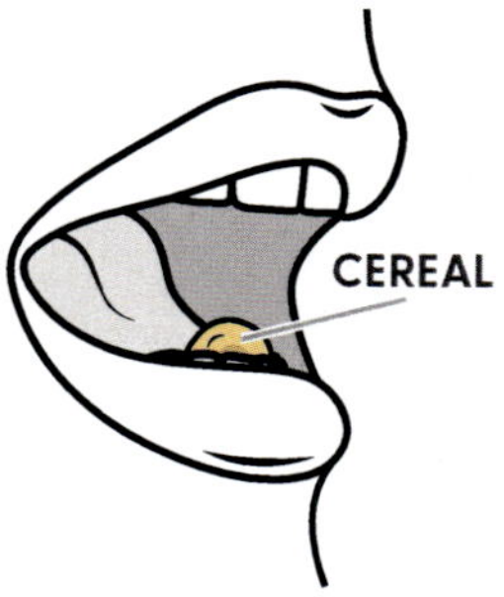

- Cereal Trick: Place a small piece of cereal (Cheerio or Froot Loop) behind the child's front bottom teeth and have them hold it with the tip of their tongue. Ask them to say the /k/ sound, keeping the cereal in place. If they lift their tongue tip to produce /t/ instead, the cereal will fall out of place. Scan the QR code for the video of this trick.
- Have the child lay back on a large physioball and have them open their mouth. Gently bounce the ball and have them practice saying /k/ on every bounce. This may encourage the tongue to fall back in the mouth.
- Alternatively, you can have the child lay on their back on the floor.
- Rename the /k/ sound. You could call it the bird sound ("caw caw"), for example.
- Have the child gargle some water to increase awareness of the back of the mouth vs. the front of the mouth.
- Touch the back of the child's neck to remind them to move the back of the tongue.
- Song to help remember /k/ placement. Lyrics: Tongue goes back to say the K, Up in back, That's the way! Tongue goes back to say the K, now lets' say our sound. Scan the QR code for the video of this song.

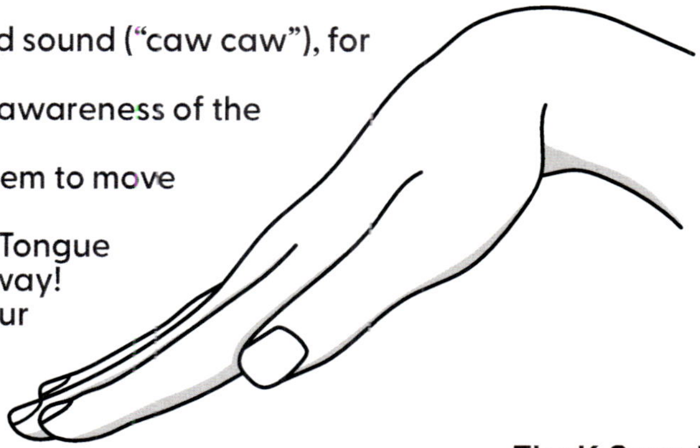

Cereal Trick

SCAN ME

The K Sound

SCAN ME

Scan these QR codes to go directly to our free videos

The G Sound

/g/

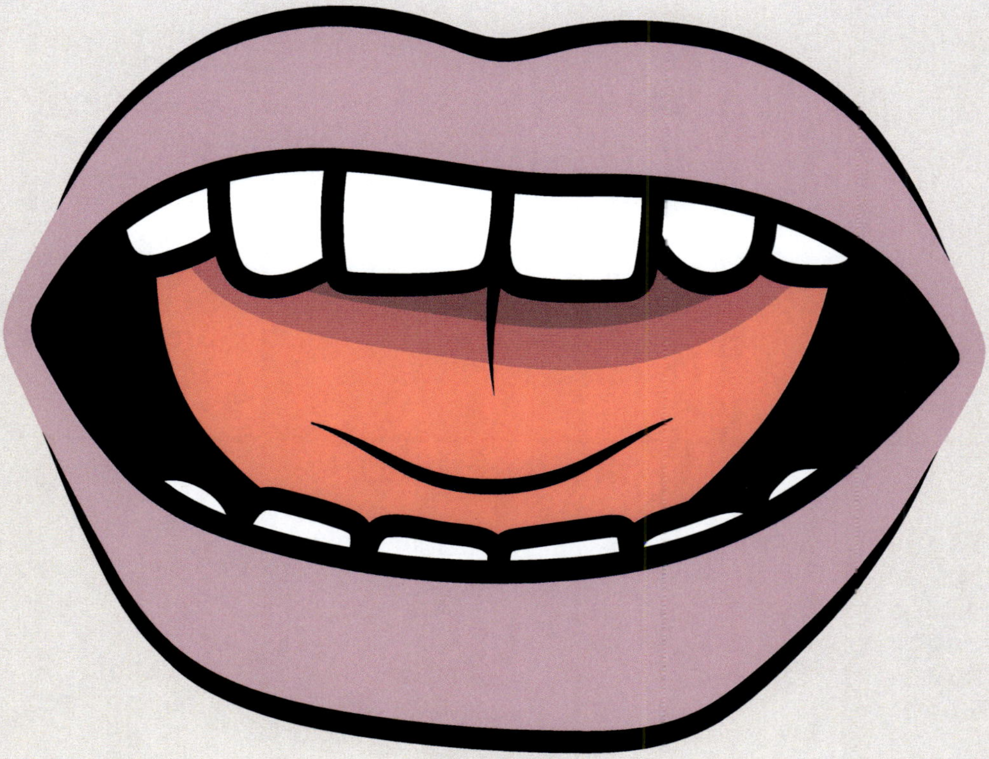

How to Say the G Sound

- Lift the back of your tongue to your soft palate.
- Release a burst of air as you turn your voice on.

PEACHIE SPEECHIE'S

Speech Sound Handbook

/g/ Word List

Initial

1 Syllable

Game
Gap
Gas
Gate
Geese
Get
Ghost
Gift
Girl
Give
Globe
Go
Goal
Goat
Gone
Good
Goof
Got
Grade
Grape
Ground
Guess
Gulp
Gum
Guy

2 Syllables

Gallon
Garage
Garlic
Gather
Gazelle
Getting
Gifted
Given
Gobble
Going
Golden
Goofy
Gopher
Gosling
Gossip
Growing
Guidance
Guilty
Guitar
Gumdrop

3 Syllables

Galaxy
Gallery
Gardening
Gasoline
Gathering
Gazebo
Getaway
Gorilla
Government
Guarantee
Guardian
Graduate
Grandfather
Grandmother
Granola
Grasshopper

Medial

Again
Agree
August
Begin
Bigger
Buggy
Burger
Cougar
Digger
Doggy
Dragon
Dugout
Eagle
Engage
Figure
Foggy
Forget
Jiggle
Jogging
Juggle
Hungry
Luggage
Magnet
Nugget
Piggy
Pigtail
Rigor
Seagull
Signal
Soggy
Sugar
Tiger
Vagus
Wagon
Yoga

Final

Bag
Big
Bug
Dog
Dug
Egg
Fig
Flag
Frog
Jog
Jug
Leg
Log
Hog
Mug
Pig
Rag
Snug
Tug
Vague
Wag
Wig

Challenge

Multiple positions within the word

Gag
Giggle
Google
Goggles
Gilligan
Eggnog
Glug

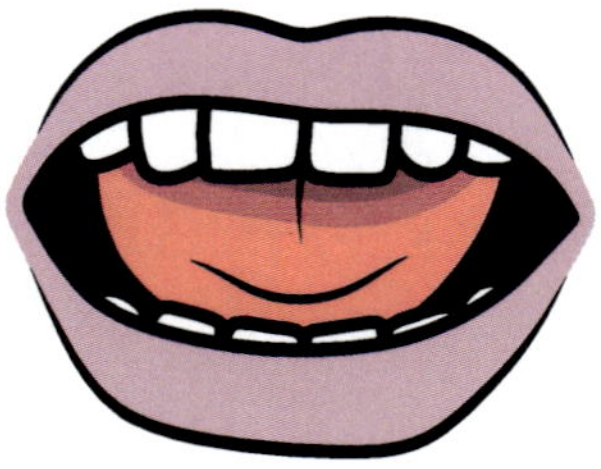

Eliciting /g/

G is a voiced velar stop sound. The back of the tongue (dorsum) lifts to touch the velum. Then, the back of the tongue quickly drops from the velum, releasing the sound. Children have typically mastered this sound by age 3.

Eliciting G

- Use a mouth model and/or illustrations to point out the velum and back of tongue to make the child aware of key articulators.
- Have the child stick their tongue out in the mirror and use a tongue depressor to point out the tip of the tongue vs. the back of the tongue. Explain that the G sound needs the back of the tongue to elevate.
- Give step-by-step placement instructions.
    1. **Lift the back of your tongue to your soft palate.**
    2. **Release a quick sound.**
- Make a tongue out of play dough and have the child lift the back of the tongue up to represent the movement required for /g/.
- Place the child's hand on your throat as you model /k/ and /g/ to demonstrate voiceless vs. voiced sounds.
- Use your thumb to touch and gently press up under the chin as they practice saying /g/.
- Use your hand to show tongue shape with the back of the hand ("tongue") elevated. Hold your hand by your throat as you model the sound.
- Gently touch the child's velum and back of tongue with a lollipop or dental swab to increase awareness of articulators.
- Touch the back of the child's neck to remind them to move the back of the tongue.
- Use a lollipop to gently push back the tongue in the mouth, and hold the tongue tip down as they practice saying /g/. This can also be done with a tongue depressor.
- Cereal Trick: Place a small piece of cereal (Cheerio or Froot Loop) behind the child's front bottom teeth and have them hold it with the tip of their tongue. Ask them to say the /g/ sound, keeping the cereal in place. If they lift their tongue tip to produce /d/ instead, the cereal will fall out of place.
- Have the child lay back on a large physioball and have them open their mouth. Gently bounce the ball and have them practice saying /g/ on every bounce. This may encourage the tongue to fall back in the mouth. Alternatively, you can have the child lay on their back on the floor.
- Rename the /g/ sound. You could call it the baby sound ("ga ga") or the drinking water sound ("gulp gulp") for example.
- Have the child gargle some water to increase awareness of the back of the mouth vs. the front of the mouth.
- Instruct the child to open their mouth wide and say /a/. Then, while they are still saying /a/ with their mouth wide open, tell them to attempt the /g/ sound while keeping their mouth in that position. Prompt them to lift the back of their tongue up to the velum. You could also start with the /i/ sound and prompt them to lift the back of the tongue up for /g/. You can ask them to do this repeatedly, which might sound like /agaga/.
- Song to help remember /g/ placement. Lyrics: The back of your tongue goes up for G, Turn your voice on, Say your sound like me. Scan the QR code for the video of this song.

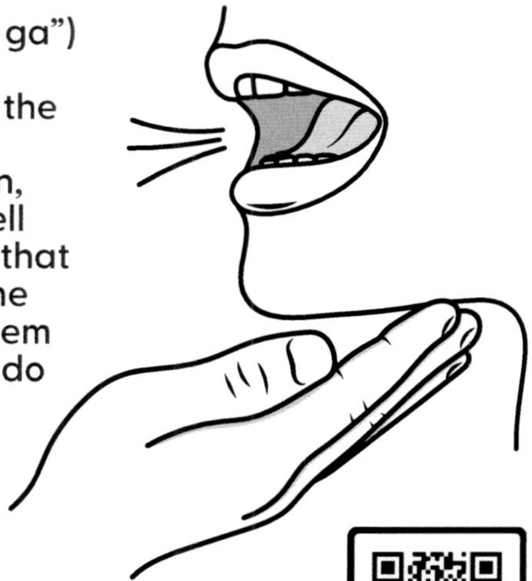

Scan this QR code to go directly to our free video

SCAN ME

The S Sound

/s/

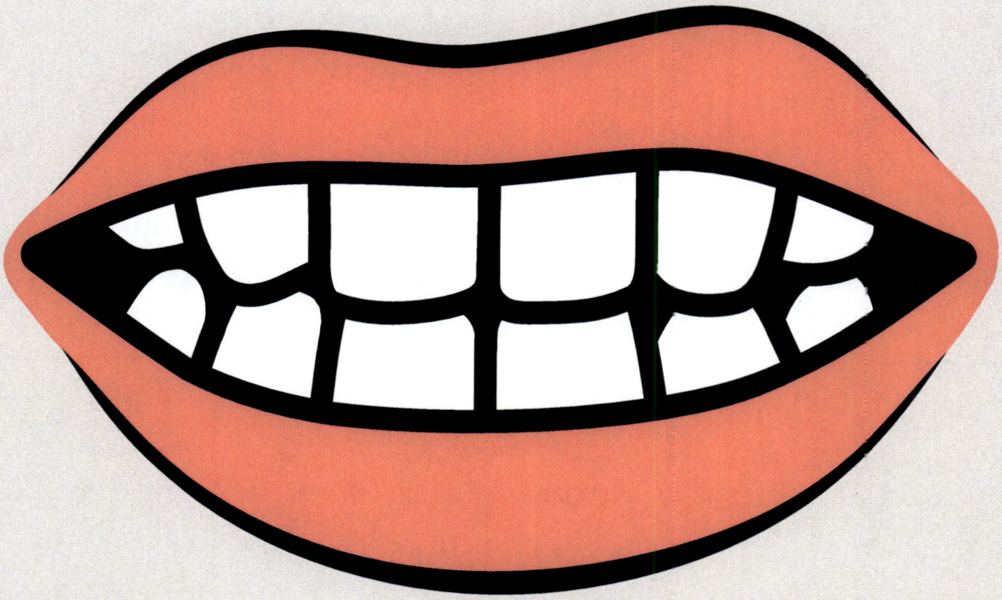

How to Say the S Sound

- Lift your tongue tip, almost touching the alveolar ridge.
- Release a stream of air over the tongue.
- Lips can be pulled back into a slight smile.
- Your voice will be off.

/s/ Word List

Initial

1 Syllable

Cell
Cent
Sack
Sad
Safe
Said
Sail
Salt
Same
Sat
Save
Sea
Search
Seat
Seed
Seem
Self
Send
Sew
Side
Sigh
Sing
Sink
Sip
Sir
Sit
Size
So
Soap
Soak
Sold
Sound
Sock
Soft
Solve
Son
Song
Soon
Sorry
Soup
Sour
South
Soy
Sub
Such
Suit
Sum
Sun
Surf

2 Syllables

Center
Cider
Circle
City
Cycle
Sadly
Safety
Sailboat
Salad
Salon
Sample
Sandal
Sandwich
Saturn
Saving
Seafood
Secret
Second
Seven
Silent
Silver
Sitting
Soapy
Soccer
Social
Soda
Sofa
Solar
Soldier
Sometime
Subject
Sunny
Super
Sushi
Syrup

3 Syllables

Celebrate
Celery
Centipede
Cereal
Cinnamon
Citizen
Cylinder
Salami
Saliva
Satellite
Saturday
Selection
Senator
Seventeen
Signature
Similar
Solution
Somebody
Suffering
Suggestion
Summary
Sunflower
Syllable
Synonym

Medial

Answer
Assign
Assume
Basic
Beside
Bicycle
Bossy
Bussing
Castle
Classic
Closer
December
Decide
Dinosaur
Dressing
Essay
Facing
Faucet
Fossil
Fussy
Gasses
Gossip
Guessing
Icy
Inside
Kissing
Lasso
Lesson
Listen
Medicine
Message
Messy
Myself
Passage
Pencil
Pieces
Possum
Pricing
Racing
Receipt
Reset
Tassel
Tossing
Tracing
Useful
Voices
Whistle

Final

Ace
Across
Base
Bonus
Bus
Cactus
Case
Class
Device
Dice
Erase
Face
Famous
Fuss
Gas
Glass
Goose
Guess
House
Ice
Juice
Kiss
Less
Lettuce
Mess
Minus
Miss
Mouse
Necklace
Nice
Pass
Peace
Place
Plus
Race
Tennis
This
Twice
Us
Voice
Yes

Challenge

Multiple positions within the word

Sickness
Science
Sister
Necessary
Success
Sixteen
Sixty
System
Silence
Sentence
Sicily

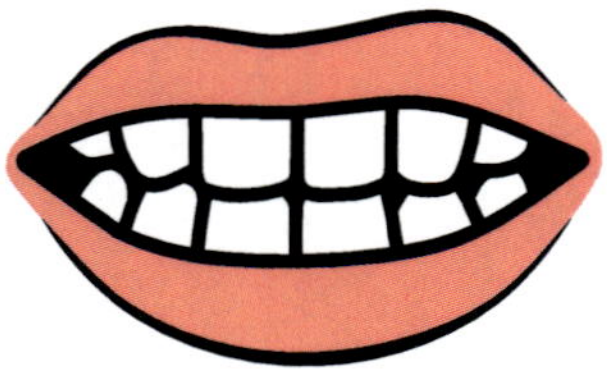

S-Blends Word List

/sn/

Snack, Snail, Snake, Snap, Sneak, Sneeze, Snip, Snooze, Snout, Snow, Snuggle

/sm/

Small, Smart, Smash, Smell, Smile, Smirk, Smock, Smoke, Smooch, Smooth, Smudge

/sp/

Space, Sparkle, Special, Speech, Spell, Spend, Spike, Spin, Spit, Sponge, Spoon, Spot, Sport, Spy

/st/

Stack, Staff, Stage, Stain, Stairs, Stamp, Stand, Star, State, Station, Stem, Stick, Stinky, Stomach, Stop, Story, Stove, Stiff, Still, Style

/sk/

Scab, Scale, Scar, Scary, School, Scoop, Scooter, Score, Scout, Skate, Ski, Skill, Skin, Skip, Skull, Skunk, Sky

/sl/

Slap, Sled, Sleep, Sleeve, Sleigh, Slicing, Slide, Slim, Slime, Slip, Slipper, Slope, Slow, Sly

/sw/

Swamp, Swan, Sway, Sweat, Swear, Sweep, Sweet, Swim, Swing, Swipe, Swirl, Switch, Swoop

Medial

Asking, Basket, History, Hospital, Mistake, Mister, Monster, Mosquito, Pasta, Poster, Whisker, Whisper, Yesterday

Final

August, Artist, Best, Biggest, Clasp, Crisp, First, Fist, Forest, Mask, Mist, Risk, Task, Taste, Toothpaste, Waist, Worst

S-Blend Tip

Have the child run their finger across the table as they sustain /s/ and then tap their finger on the table for the next sound in the blend. You can also use a visual like the one pictured below.

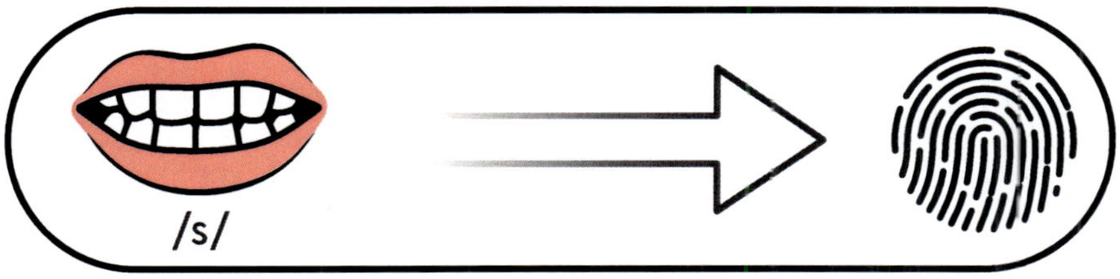

S-Blends

SCAN ME

Scan this QR code to go directly to our free video

Eliciting /s/

S is a lingua-alveolar voiceless fricative sound. The blade and/or tip of the tongue lifts up to almost touch the alveolar ridge. The sides of the tongue elevate as well, touching the insides of the molars. Air flows straight through the midline groove in the tongue to produce the /s/ sound. Children have typically mastered this sound by age 4.

Note that some people produce /s/ with their tongue tip up, and others produce it with their blade up and tongue tip pointed down.

Eliciting S

- Use a mouth model and/or illustrations to point out the parts of the tongue (tip, blade) and alveolar ridge to make the child aware of key articulators.
- Make a tongue out of play-dough and demonstrate placement in a mouth model.
- Give step-by-step placement instructions.
    1. **Lift your tongue tip up to touch your alveolar ridge.**
    2. **Make sure the sides of your tongue are up touching the insides of your teeth as well.**
    3. **Pull your tongue tip back a little bit from your alveolar ridge so air can flow straight forward, making the /s/ sound.**
- Remind the child to keep their tongue inside their teeth. "Don't let your tongue escape!"
- Tell the child to gently bite, smile, and blow air straight forward.
- Discuss "stop sounds" vs. "go sounds". Stop sounds are quick like /t/, /d/, and /p/, but "go sounds" can go on and on like /s/, /z/, /ʃ/, /m/ etc. Tell them to hold out /s/ and make it long.
- Rename /s/. Call it the teapot sound or the snake sound as you instruct the child on proper tongue placement.
- During production of a frontal lisp, the jaw drops. Let the child touch under your chin as you produce the /s/ sound and then the /θ/ sound so they can feel the jaw dropping. Remind them to keep their tongue inside their teeth to avoid jaw dropping.
- Use a lollipop or dental swab to rub the alveolar ridge to increase awareness. Instruct the child to lift their tongue tip up to where you touched. You can also rub the lateral margins of the tongue and prompt them to lift the sides of the tongue up to the insides of the teeth.
- Point to the outside edges of the mouth and make a pinching motion with your thumb and index finger to remind the child to keep the jaw in a high position with lips spread.
- Shape from the F sound: Instruct the child to produce the /f/ sound but make it very gentle, with the teeth barely reaching the bottom lip. Make it extra breathy. Then, while they sustain airflow, have them lift their tongue tip up to transform the /f/ into an /s/.

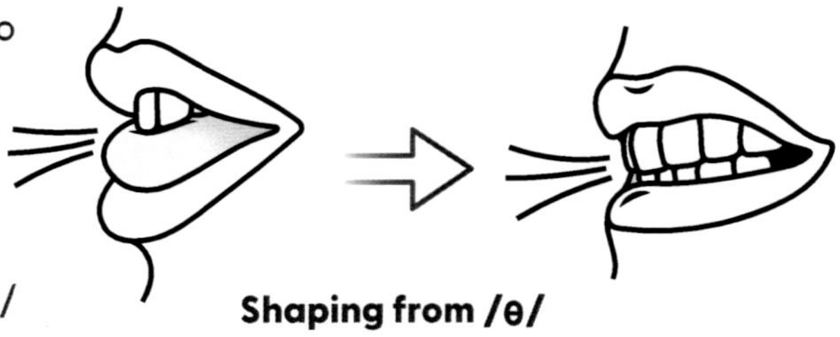

Shaping from /θ/

- Shape from the TH sound: Have the child start with /θ/ and then while they sustain airflow, pull the tongue back into the mouth.
- Shape from the H Sound: Have the child say the /h/ sound and then while continuing to sustain the sound, close the jaw and bring the tongue tip/blade up.
- Shape from the L sound: Instruct the child to lift their tongue tip up and say /l/. Tell them to keep their tongue in the L position and then close their teeth and blow air straight over their tongue. The tongue tip will drop a little to allow air to flow out.
- Instruct the child to make a "stretched out /t/" with extra air. As they hold out the /t/ sound, it can turn into an /s/ sound.
- If the child can make a /z/ sound, tell them to turn their voice off and make a whispered /z/ to achieve /s/.
- Song to help remember /s/ placement with tongue behind teeth. Lyrics: Teeth are close with your tongue inside, air slides out, sssssss. Scan the QR code for the video of this song.

SCAN ME

Scan this QR code to go directly to our free video

PEACHIE SPEECHIE'S

Speech Sound Handbook

Tips for Lateral /s/

- Discuss tongue placement for both correct /s/ and lateral /s/. Correct /s/ has the lateral margins of the tongue lifted so air can flow straight forward down the tongue. Lateral /s/ has the lateral margins of the tongue lowered, with the center of the tongue elevated.
- Show visuals to illustrate the differences in tongue placement.
- Make a tongue out of play dough and lift the lateral margins and tongue tip to demonstrate correct placement. You can also show incorrect placement to help them visualize the difference.
- Stretchy T: Have the child repeat the /t/ sound (T-T-T-T) and then tell them to hold out the T sound and make it stretchy (T-T-T-TSsss). You can scan the QR code below to see a video of this technique in action.
- Rename the /s/ sound. Call it the Stretchy T as mentioned above, or the air sound or hissing sound, for example.
- Select target words that have /ts/ sound in them to facilitate placement and forward airflow. For example: goats, hats, cuts.
- If the child has jaw sliding, you can stabilize the jaw using a bite block, tongue depressor or thin straw. Hold the bite block between the molars as they practice producing forward airflow for /s/.
- Hold a drinking straw up to the mouth, near the lips, as the child produces the /s/ sound. If they are using forward airflow, you will hear air rushing through the straw when it's positioned directly in front of of their front teeth. If they have lateral airflow, you'll hear air rushing through the straw when it's held at the side of the mouth.

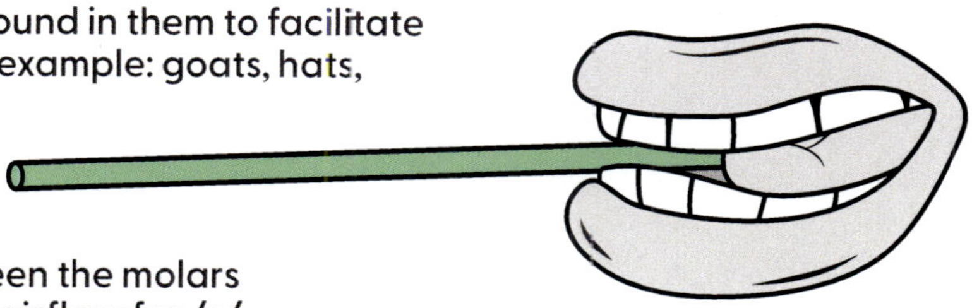

Lateral S

center of tongue lifted

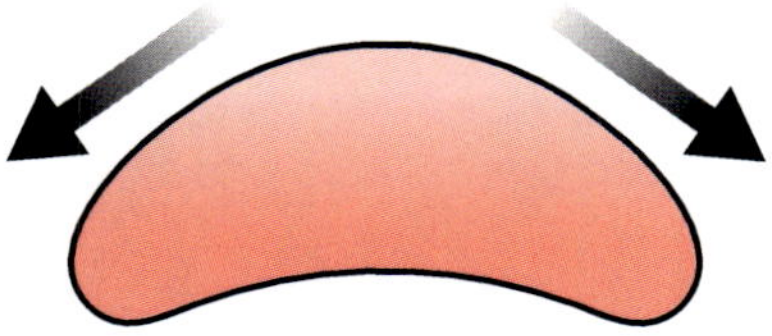

air flows over the sides of the tongue

Correct S

sides of tongue lifted

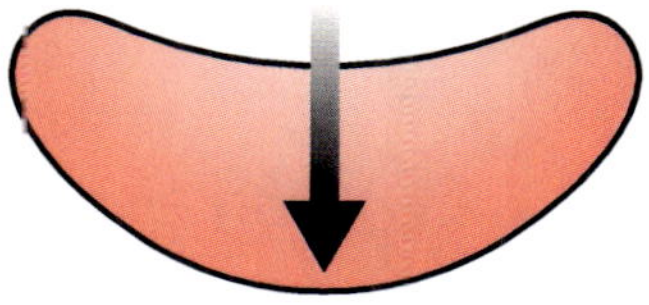

air flows straight down the midline groove

Stretchy T

SCAN ME

PEACHIE SPEECHIE'S

Speech Sound Handbook

The Z Sound

/z/

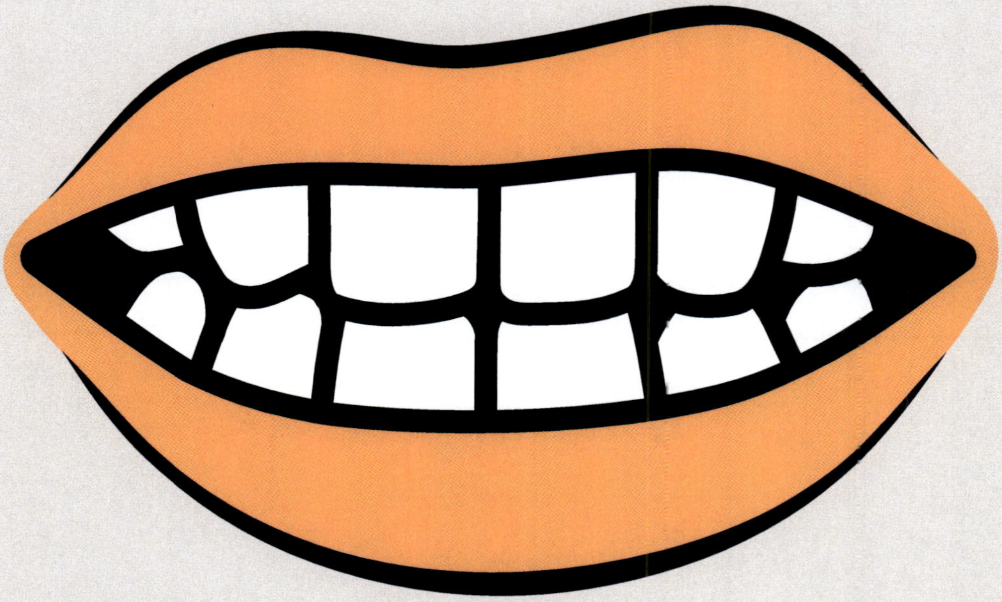

How to Say the Z Sound

- Lift your tongue tip, almost touching the alveolar ridge.
- Release a stream of air over the tongue.
- Lips can be pulled back into a slight smile.
- Your voice will be on.

PEACHIE SPEECHIE'S

Speech Sound Handbook

/z/ Word List

Initial

1 Syllable	*2 Syllables*	*3 Syllables*
Czar	Zany	Xylophone
Zag	Zealous	Zachary
Zap	Zebra	Zambia
Zeal	Zelda	Zeroing
Zee	Zero	Zestfully
Zen	Zestful	Zinnia
Zest	Zeta	Zodiac
Zeus	Zillion	Zucchini
Zinc	Zipper	
Zing	Zither	
Zip	Zombie	
Zone	Zoning	
Zoo	Zorro	
Zoom		

Medial

Asthma	Easy	Tuesday
Blazer	Freezer	User
Blizzard	Frozen	Visit
Breezy	Fuzzy	Wasn't
Busy	Housing	Wizard
Cheesy	Isn't	
Closet	Lizard	
Cousin	Noisy	
Cozy	Oozing	
Crazy	Present	
Daisy	Puzzle	
Dazzle	Raisin	
Design	Razor	
Dessert	Resort	
Dizzy	Season	
Dozen	Thousand	
Easel	Thursday	

Final

As	Fries	Please
Bees	Froze	Prize
Boys	Goes	Quiz
Bruise	Has	Rise
Buzz	He's	Says
Cause	Is	Sees
Cheese	Jazz	She's
Choose	Keys	Shoes
Clothes	Knees	Sneeze
Clues	Lies	Those
Cries	News	Toes
Days	Noise	Toys
Does	Nose	Tries
Dries	Ones	Use
Ease	Pause	Was
Eyes	Peas	Ways
Fizz	Pies	

Challenge

Multiple positions within the word

Buzzes
Scissors
Mazes
Houses
Measles
Zigzag

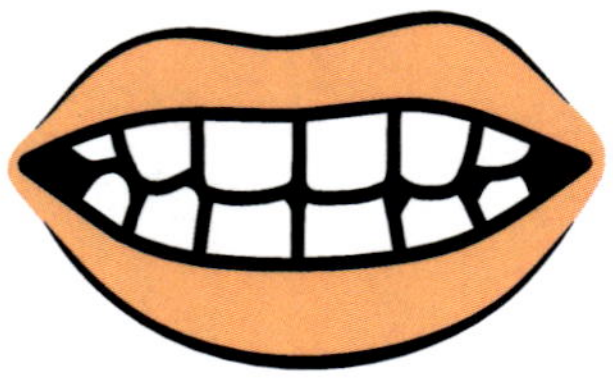

Eliciting /z/

Z is a lingua-alveolar voiced fricative sound. The blade and/or tip of the tongue lifts up to almost touch the alveolar ridge. The sides of the tongue elevate as well, touching the insides of the molars. Air flows straight through the midline groove in the tongue with the voice on to produce the /z/ sound. Children have typically mastered this sound by age 4.

Note that some people produce /z/ with their tongue tip up, and others produce it with their blade up and tongue tip pointed down.

Eliciting Z

- Use a mouth model and/or illustrations to point out the parts of the tongue (tip, blade) and alveolar ridge to make the child aware of key articulators.
- Make a tongue out of play-dough and demonstrate placement in a plastic mouth model.
- Give step-by-step placement instructions.
    1. Lift your tongue tip up to touch your alveolar ridge.
    2. Make sure the sides of your tongue are up touching the insides of your teeth as well.
    3. Pull your tongue tip back a little bit from your alveolar ridge so air can flow straight forward with your voice on, making the /z/ sound.
- Remind them to keep their tongue inside their teeth. "Don't let your tongue escape!"
- Tell the child to gently bite, smile, and blow air straight forward with their voiced turned on.
- Discuss "stop sounds" vs. "go sounds". Stop sounds are quick like /t/, /d/, and /p/ but "go sounds" can go on and on like /s/, /z/, /ʃ/, /m/ etc. Tell them to hold out /z/ and make it long.
- Rename /z/. Call it the buzzing sound or the zipping sound as you instruct the child on proper tongue placement.
- Have the child place their hand on your throat as you produce /s/ and /z/ to draw attention to the voicing of the /z/ sound.
- During production of a frontal lisp, the jaw drops. Let the child touch under your chin as you produce the /z/ sound and then the /ð/ sound so they can feel the jaw dropping. Remind them to keep their tongue inside their teeth to avoid jaw dropping.
- Use a lollipop or dental swab to rub the alveolar ridge to increase awareness. Instruct the child to lift their tongue tip up to where you touched. You can also rub the lateral margins of the tongue and prompt them to lift the sides of the tongue up to the insides of the teeth.
- Point to the outside edges of the mouth and make a pinching motion with your thumb and index finger to remind the child to keep the jaw in a high position with lips spread. Touch or point to your throat to remind them to turn their voice on.
- Instruct the child to produce the /i/ sound and then slowly close their jaw and lift their tongue tip up while they sustain the sound. This will turn /i/ into /z/. You can have them transition back into the /i/ sound, so it sounds like they are saying the word, "easy", /izi/.

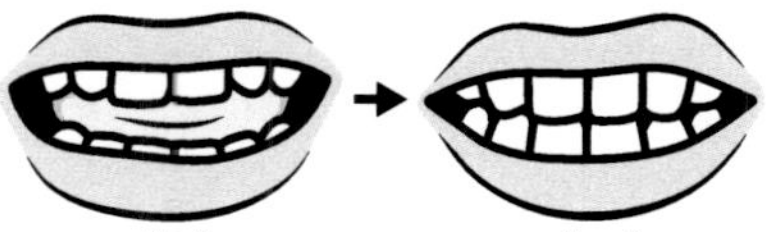

- Shape from the voiced TH sound: Have the child start with /ð/ and then while they sustain the sound, pull the tongue back into the mouth.
- Instruct the child to make a "stretched out /d/". As they hold out the /d/ sound, it can turn into a /z/ sound.
- Fast D to Z: Instruct your student to say the /d/ sound quickly and repeatedly and then tell them to hold out the sound. It will sound like dzzzzzz.
- If the child can make a /s/ sound, tell them to turn their voice on and make a "loud /s/" to achieve /z/.

Scan this QR code to go directly to our free video

SCAN ME

PEACHIE SPEECHIE'S

Speech Sound Handbook

The F Sound

/f/

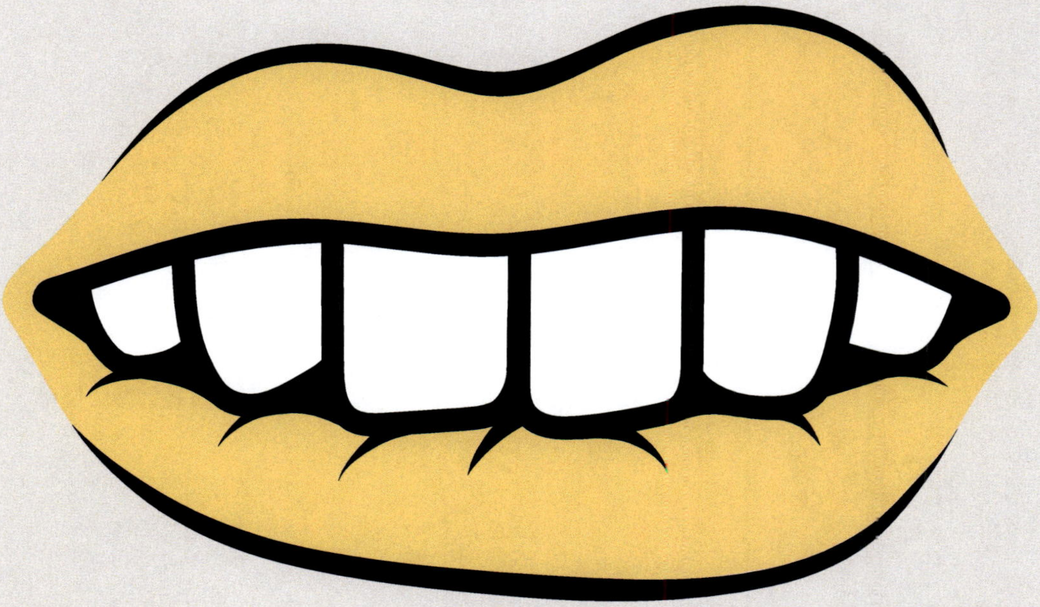

How to Say the F Sound

- Put your upper teeth on your lower lip and blow air over your lip.
- Keep your voice off.

PEACHIE SPEECHIE'S

Speech Sound Handbook

/f/ Word List

Initial

1 Syllable

Face
Fact
Fair
Fall
Fan
Far
Farm
Fast
Fat
Fear
Feed
Feel
Fell
Fence
Fetch
Fig
Fill
Fin
Find
Fire
First
Fish
Five
Fix
Fog
Food
For
Fork
Fort
Four
Full
Fun
Fuss
Phone

2 Syllables

Faces
Fairy
Famous
Fancy
Farmer
Father
Faucet
Favor
Feather
Fellow
Female
Fiction
Fidget
Figure
Final
Finger
Finish
Fishing
Fitness
Football
Foreign
Fourteen
Funny
Pharynx
Phoneme
Phonics
Photo

3 Syllables

Factory
Family
Fantasy
Federal
Feminine
Festival
Fingernail
Florida
Follower
Forever
Formula
Furniture
Pharmacist
Phobia
Physical
Physician

Medial

Awful
Before
Bonfire
Cafe
Careful
Caffeine
Coffee
Defend
Different
Effect
Goldfish
Gopher
Graphic
Headphone
Infant
Joyful
Laughing
Muffin
Offend
Official
Outfit
Playful
Puffy
Safety
Sofa
Seafood
Suffix
Traffic
Trophy
Wishful

Final

Beef
Calf
Chef
Cough
Deaf
Enough
Giraffe
Goof
Half
If
Knife
Laugh
Leaf
Life
Loaf
Off
Puff
Relief
Roof
Rough
Safe
Self
Staff
Stuff
Wife
Wolf
Woof

Challenge

Multiple positions within the word

Firefly
Firefighter
Frankfurter
Flameproof
Flagstaff
Faithful
Forceful

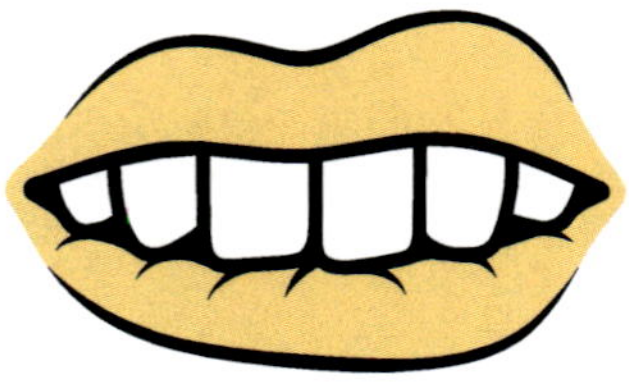

Eliciting /f/

F is a voiceless labiodental fricative. The upper teeth contact the lower lip. Constricted air is blown over the lip to produce the /f/ sound. Children have typically mastered this sound by age 3.

Eliciting F

- Use a mirror to point out articulators in your mouth and the childs. You can also use printed visuals to teach key articulators, focusing on the lower lip and upper teeth for /f/.
- Rub the inner half of the lower lip with a lollipop or dental swab to increase awareness. Then, instruct them to bring the lower lip to touch the upper teeth for /f/.
- Give step-by-step placement instructions.
    1. Rest your upper teeth on your lower lip.
    2. Blow quiet air over your lip to make the /f/ sound.
- Smile and Bite: Tell the child to smile wide with their mouth open a little bit. Then, tell them to close their smile and gently bite their lower lip. Then, tell them to let air straight out for /f/.
- Place a finger (either yours, or the child's) under their lower lip. Lift the finger up, supporting the bottom lip until it meets the upper teeth. Keeping the finger in place, instruct them to release a stream of air over the lip. This air can be felt hitting the finger as well.
- Rename the /f/ sound. Call it the fan sound, the windy sound, or the lip sound as you instruct the child on proper placement.
- Shape from the H sound. Have the child sustain the /h/ sound as they bring their bottom lip up to the top teeth. Keep the air flowing as the sound changes from an H to an F.
- Shape from the P sound. Instruct the child to bring their lips together for the /p/ sound, but make it a "long P sound", releasing a slow stream of air through the lips instead of saying a regular /p/. Tell them to keep blowing air as they curl their bottom lip in to meet the upper teeth.
- If the child can say the /v/ sound, tell them to make a "Quiet V" to achieve an accurate /f/
- Song to help remember placement for /f/. Lyrics: Lip goes in, Tiny Bite, Blow the air for the F sound. Scan the QR code for the video of this song.

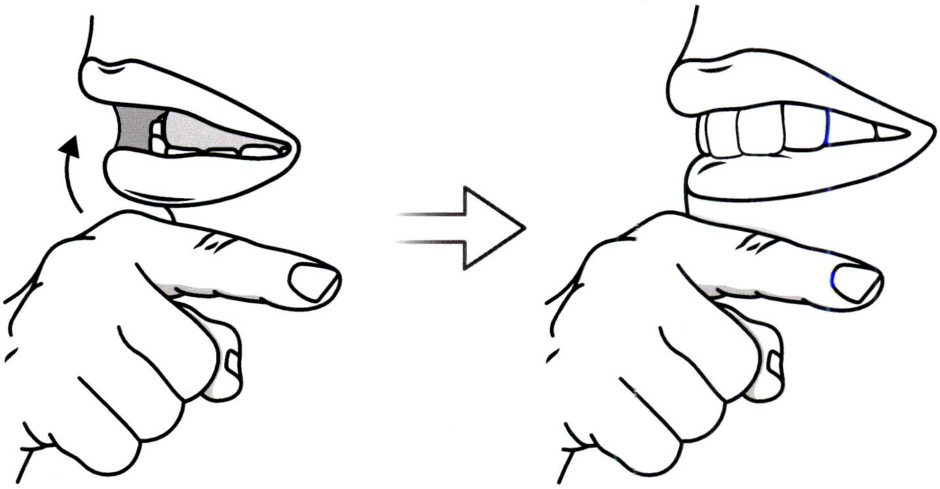

Scan this QR code to go directly to our free video

SCAN ME

The V Sound

/v/

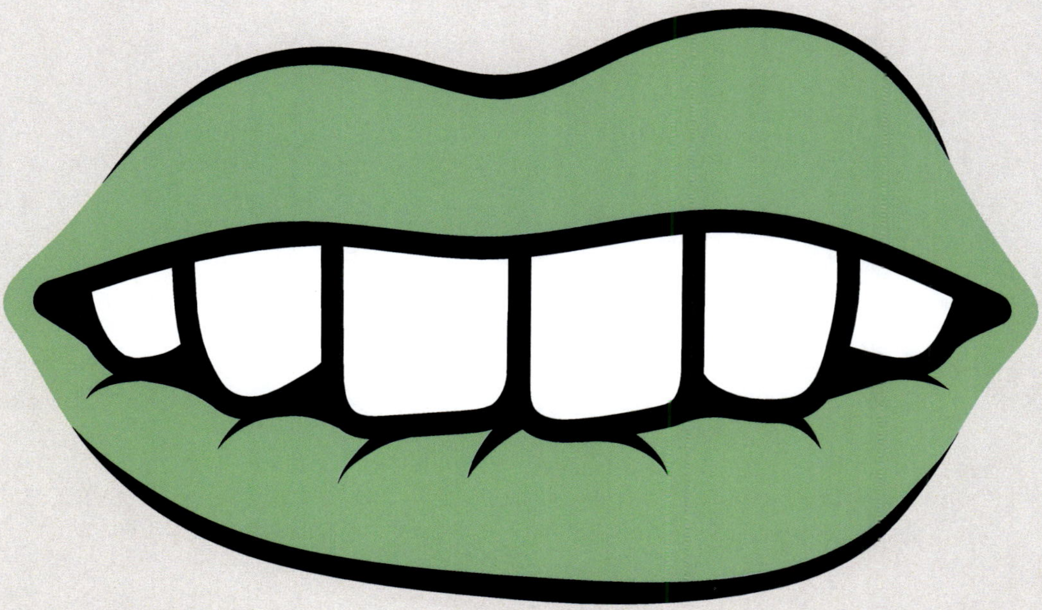

How to Say the V Sound

- Put your upper teeth on your lower lip and blow air over your lip.
- Keep your voice on.

PEACHIE SPEECHIE'S

Speech Sound Handbook

/v/ Word List

Initial

1 Syllable

Vague
Van
Vase
Vat
Vault
Vein
Vent
Verb
Verse
Vest
Vet
Vex
Vine
Voice
Void
Vote
Vow

2 Syllables

Vaccine
Vacuum
Valid
Valley
Value
Vampire
Vanish
Vapor
Vary
Venom
Venus
Verdict
Version
Versus
Village
Viper
Virus
Visit
Vision
Visor
Vocal
Volley
Volume
Vowel
Voyage

3 Syllables

Vacation
Valentine
Vampire
Vanilla
Varsity
Vegetable
Vehicle
Verify
Vertical
Vibration
Video
Violet
Violin
Virginia
Visitor
Volcano
Volleyball
Voyager

Medial

Adverb
Advertise
Advice
Avoid
Beaver
Canvas
Carnival
Clever
Convex
Convince
Develop
Device
Diver
Envelope
Even
Every
Event
Favor
Given
Haven't
Having
Heavy
Inventing
Lava
Leaving
Loving
Moving
Navy
Never
Novel
November
Over
Private
Raven
Revise
Seven
Silver
Travel
Waving

Final

Achieve
Believe
Beehive
Brave
Cave
Concave
Cursive
Dive
Drive
Eve
Five
Gave
Give
Glove
Have
Hive
Improve
I've
Leave
Live
Love
Microwave
Move
Native
Olive
Remove
Save
Shove
Skydive
Sleeve
Stove
They've
Thrive
Wave
We've
You've

Challenge

Multiple positions within the word

Valve
Velvet
Vivian
Vivid
Vivacious

Eliciting /v/

V is a voiced labiodental fricative. The upper teeth contact the lower lip. Constricted air is blown over the lip with the voice turned on to produce the /v/ sound. Children have typically mastered this sound by age 4.

Eliciting V

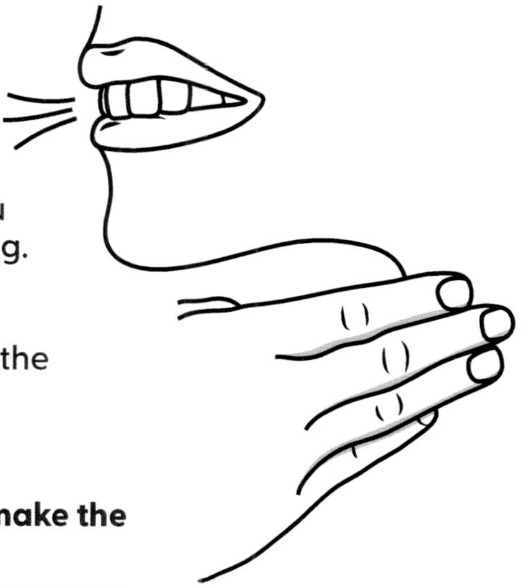

- Use a mirror to point out articulators in your mouth and the childs. You can also use printed visuals to teach key articulators, focusing on the lower lip and upper teeth for /v/.
- Instruct the child to place their hand on your throat as you say the /f/ and the /v/ sounds to draw attention to voicing. Tell them the V sound uses their voice.
- Rub the inner half of the lower lip with a lollipop or dental swab to increase awareness. Then, instruct them to bring the lower lip to touch the upper teeth for /v/.
- Give step-by-step placement instructions.
  1. **Gently rest your upper teeth on your lower lip.**
  2. **Turn your voice on as you blow air over your lip to make the /v/ sound.**
- Smile and Bite: Tell the child to smile wide with their mouth open a little bit. Then, tell them to close their smile and gently bite their lower lip. Then, tell them to turn on their voice and let air straight out for /v/.
- Place a finger (either yours, or the child's) under their lower lip. Lift the finger up, supporting the bottom lip until it meets the upper teeth. Keeping the finger in place, instruct them to release a voiced stream of air over the lip. This air can be felt hitting the finger as well.
- Rename the /v/ sound. Call it the vroom-vroom car sound or the buzzing lip sound as you instruct the child on proper placement.
- Shape from the AH sound. Have the child sustain the /a/ sound as they bring their bottom lip up to the top teeth. Keep the sound going as the sound changes from an AH to a V.
- You HAVE the V Sound. Start by instructing the child to say /hæ/, sustaining the /æ/ sound. While continuing the /æ/ sound, instruct them to curl their bottom lip in to meet the top teeth. This will sound like they are slowly saying the word "have".
- Shape from the B sound. Instruct the child to bring their lips together for the /b/ sound, but make it a "long B sound", releasing a slow stream of voiced air through the lips instead of saying a regular /b/. Tell them to keep the sound going as they curl their bottom lip in to meet the upper teeth.
- If the child can say the /f/ sound, tell them to make a "Loud F" to achieve an accurate /v/.
- You can ask the child to put their hand over their own throat to feel the vibration of the /v/ sound.
- Song to help remember placement for /v/. Lyrics: Little bite on your lip, turn on your voice /v/-/v/! Little bite on your lip, turn on your voice /v/-/v/! Blow your air over your lip, now you've got the hang of it, Little bite on your lip, turn on your voice /v/-/v/! Scan the QR code for the video of this song.

Scan this QR code to go directly to our free video

SCAN ME

The TH Sound (Voiceless) /θ/

How to Say the TH Sound (Voiceless)

- **Put your tongue between your teeth and blow air between your tongue and teeth.**
- **Keep your voice turned off.**

PEACHIE SPEECHIE'S

Speech Sound Handbook

/θ/ Word List

Initial

1 Syllable

Thank
Thatch
Thaw
Theft
Theme
Thick
Thigh
Thin
Thing
Think
Third
Thirst
Throw
Thread
Throat
Thor
Thorn
Thought
Thud
Thumb
Thump

2 Syllables

Thankful
Thermos
Thesis
Theta
Thicken
Thinking
Thinner
Thirteen
Thirty
Thorax
Thousand
Thumbnail
Thumbtack
Thunder
Thursday

3 Syllables

Thanksgiving
Theater
Thematic
Theodore
Therapist
Therapy
Thermostat
Thesaurus
Thunderbolt
Thunderstorm

Medial

Athlete
Author
Bathmat
Bathtub
Birthday
Earthquake
Ethics
Healthy
Method
Mouthful
Nothing
Pathway
Playthings
Python
Southeast
Toothache
Toothpaste
Truthful
Wealthy
Withdraw
Within
Without
Youthful

Final

Bath
Birth
Both
Breath
Cloth
Death
Earth
Faith
Health
Length
Math
Mouth
Month
North
Path
Seventh
Sloth
South
Strength
Teeth
Tenth
Truth
Warmth
Wreath
Youth

Challenge

Multiple positions within the word

Thirty-three

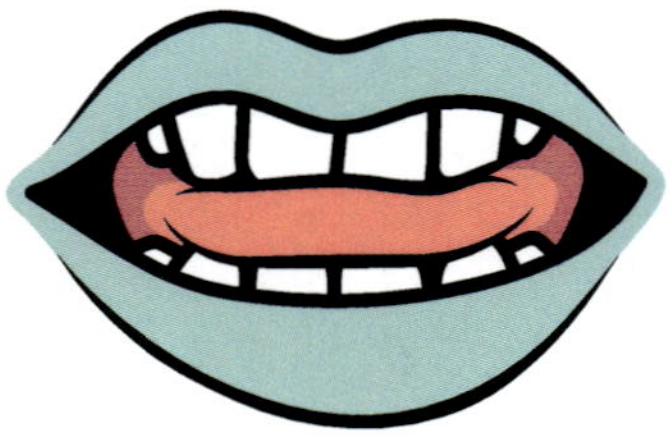

PEACHIE SPEECHIE'S

Speech Sound Handbook

Eliciting /θ/

TH is a voiceless lingua-dental fricative. The tip of the tongue protrudes slightly through the teeth. It lightly touches the bottom edges of the front teeth as an unvoiced airstream is directed forward. Children have typically mastered this sound by age 4.

Eliciting Voiceless TH

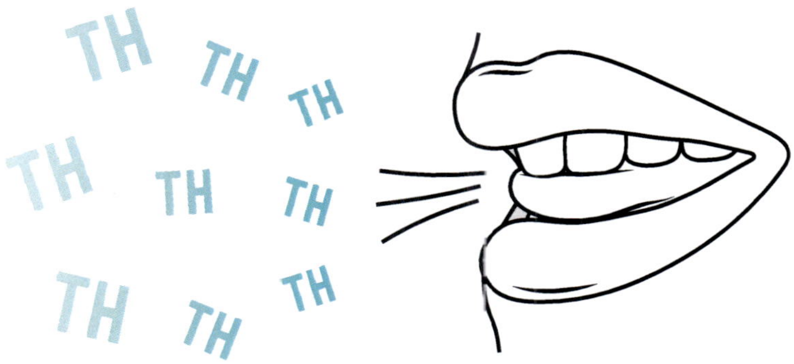

- Teach basic anatomy of the mouth, focusing on tongue tip and teeth for the TH sound.
- Model how to say the TH sound to your student and ask them to imitate in the mirror.
- Give step-by-step placement instructions.
    1. **Open your mouth just a little bit.**
    2. **Place your tongue between your teeth.**
    3. **Blow air down your tongue between your teeth.**
    4. **Remember to keep your voice off, since TH is a quiet sound.**
- Shape from the S Sound. Instruct the child to say /s/ and then while sustaining airflow, slowly bring the tongue tip forward between the teeth. Listen as the S sound turns into the TH sound.
- Shape from the H sound. Start by asking the child to say the /h/ sound. Instruct them to sustain airflow as they bring their tongue forward between their teeth and close their jaw a little bit. Listen as the H sound turns into the TH sound.
- Shape from the F sound. Start by asking the child to say the F sound. Have them sustain airflow for /f/ as they bring their tongue tip forward between their teeth. Listen as the F sound turns into the TH sound.
- If the child is sticking their tongue out too far (overprotrusion), you can hold a dental swab, straw, or tongue depressor in front of their lips and tell them not to let their tongue touch the item.
- If the child is not sticking their tongue out enough, you can tell them to smile big and then place a lollipop just outside their teeth. Ask them to keep smiling and bring just the tip of their tongue out to touch the lollipop. Once in position, ask them to release air straight forward.
- For children saying /f/ instead of /θ/, you can call /f/ the "lip sound" and /θ/ the "tongue sound". Use a mirror and say, "Show me your tongue for the tongue sound".
- Rename the TH sound. Call it the tongue-sandwich sound or the leaky air sound as you give placement instructions.
- Song to help remember placement for /θ/ Lyrics: Put your tongue between your teeth just like this /θ/-/θ/. Put your tongue between your teeth just like this /θ/-/θ/. You'll blow the air right out, it's a quiet sound don't shout, Put your tongue between your teeth just like this /θ/-/θ/. Scan the QR code for the video of this song.

Scan this QR code to go directly to our free video

SCAN ME

The TH Sound (Voiced) /ð/

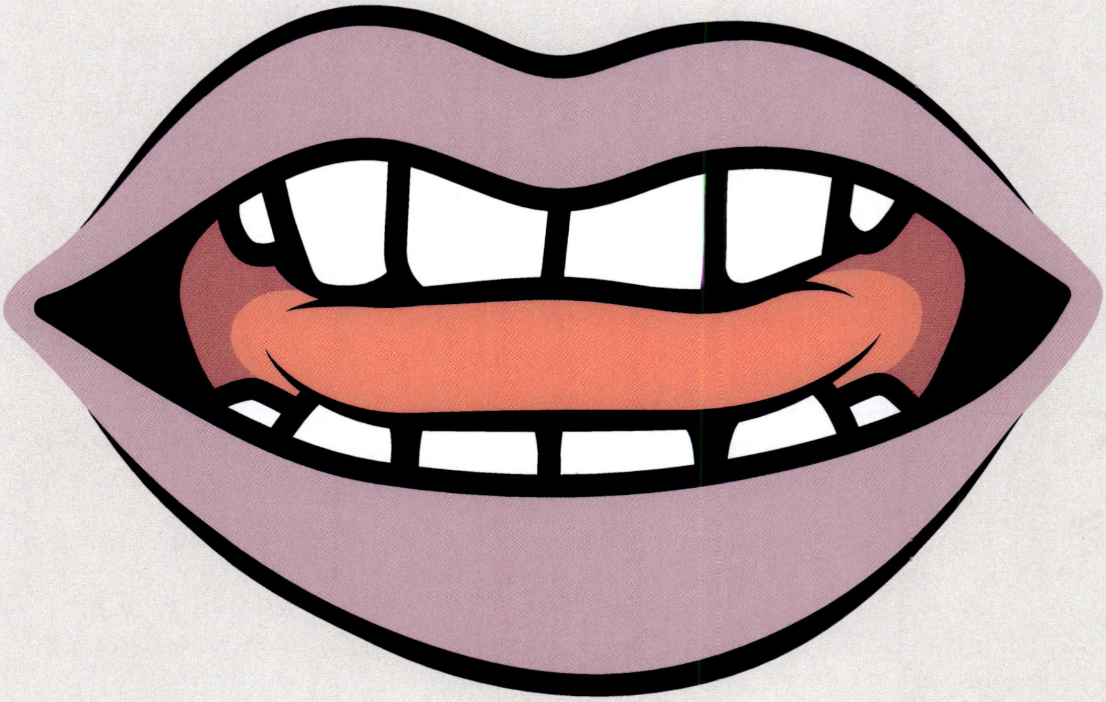

How to Say the TH Sound (Voiced)

- Put your tongue between your teeth and blow air between your tongue and teeth.
- Turn your voice on.

PEACHIE SPEECHIE'S

Speech Sound Handbook

/ð/ Word List

Initial

1 Syllable

Than
That
The
Their
Them
Then
These
They
They'd
This
Those
Though
Thus
Thy

2 Syllables

Themselves
Thereby
Therefore
Thereof
Thyself

3 Syllables

Thereabout
Thereafter

3 Syllable Phrases

Those people
These candies
That's because
They're friendly
They've seen us
This subject

Medial

Although
Another
Bathing
Bother
Breathing
Brother
Clothing
Either
Farther
Feather
Gather
Leather
Mother
Neither
Other
Otherwise
Rather
Smoother
Southern
Tetherball
Together
Weather

Final

Bathe
Breathe
Clothe
Smooth
Soothe
Teethe

Challenge Phrases

Multiple positions within the word

Leather clothing
Southern leather
Soothing rhythm
The grandfathers
Those brothers
Northern weather

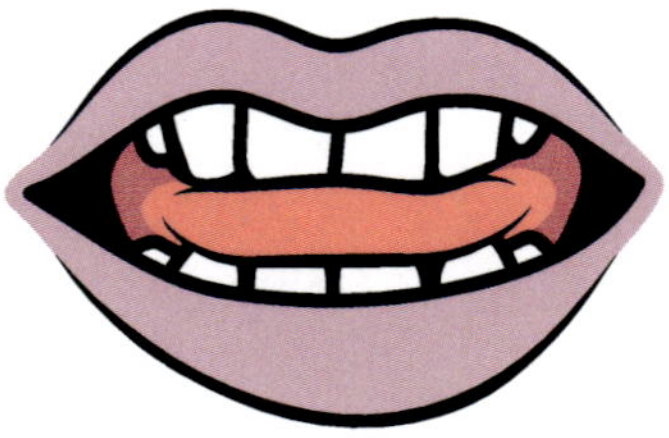

Eliciting /ð/

TH is a voiced lingua-dental fricative. The tip of the tongue protrudes slightly through the teeth. It lightly touches the bottom edges of the front teeth as a voiced airstream is directed forward. Children have typically mastered this sound by age 6.

Eliciting Voiced TH

- Teach basic anatomy of the mouth, focusing on tongue tip and teeth for the TH sound.
- Model how to say the TH sound to your student and ask them to imitate in the mirror.
- Give step-by-step placement instructions.
  1. **Open your mouth just a little bit.**
  2. **Place your tongue between your teeth.**
  3. **Blow air down the tongue between your teeth.**
  4. **Turn your voice on, since TH is a noisy (voiced) sound.**
- Have the child place their hand on your throat as you model both voiceless and voiced TH to draw attention to the voicing needed for /ð/.
- Shape from the Z Sound. Instruct the child to say /z/ and then while sustaining airflow, slowly bring the tongue tip forward between the teeth. Listen as the /z/ sound turns into the /ð/ sound.
- Shape from the /a/ sound. Start by asking the child to say the /a/ sound. Instruct them to sustain airflow as they bring their tongue forward between their teeth and close their jaw a little bit. Listen as the /a/ sound turns into the /ð/ sound.
- Shape from the V sound. Start by asking the child to say the /v/ sound. Have them sustain airflow for /v/ as they bring their tongue tip forward between his teeth. Listen as the /v/ sound turns into the /ð/ sound.
- Shape from the EE sound. Start by asking the child to hold out the /i/ sound. Then, tell them to slowly slide their tongue forward between their teeth, keeping the airflow going. As they gently touch the tongue tip to the upper teeth, they will hear their sound change.
- If the child is sticking their tongue out too far (overprotrusion), you can hold a dental swab, straw, or tongue depressor in front of their lips and tell them not to let their tongue touch the item.
- If the child is not sticking their tongue out enough, you can tell them to smile big and then place a lollipop just outside their teeth. Ask them to keep smiling and bring just the tip of their tongue out to touch the lollipop. Once in position, ask them to release the sound straight forward.
- For children saying /v/ instead of /ð/, you can call /v/ the "lip sound" and /ð/ the "tongue sound". Use a mirror and say "Show me your tongue for the tongue sound".
- Rename the TH sound. Call it the tongue-sandwich sound or the tongue buzzing sound as you give placement instructions.

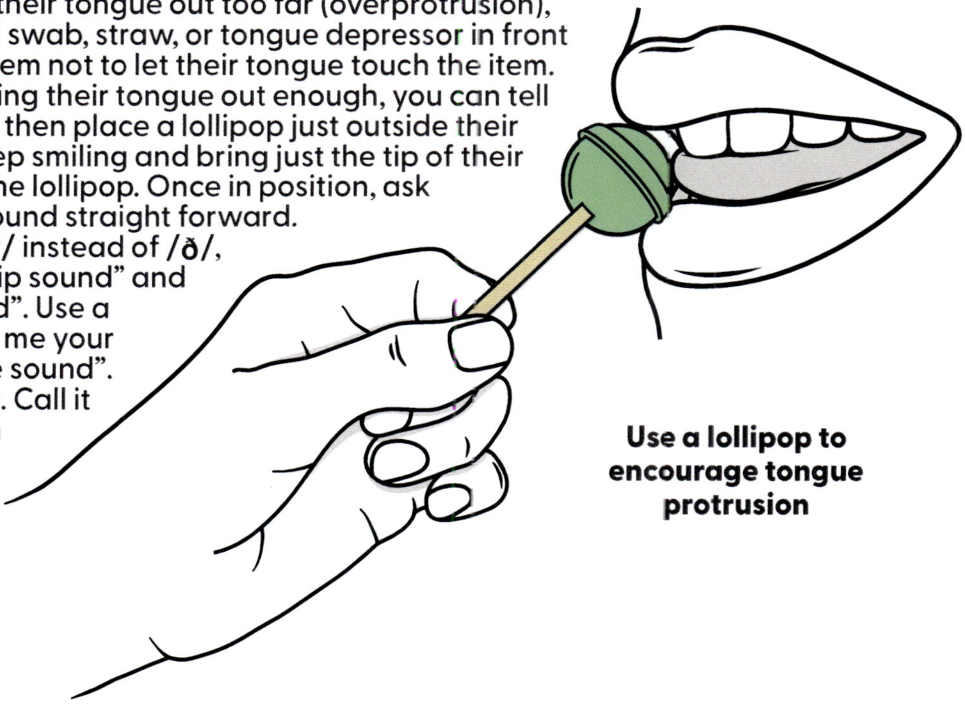

Use a lollipop to encourage tongue protrusion

PEACHIE SPEECHIE'S

Speech Sound Handbook

The SH Sound

/ʃ/

How to Say the SH Sound

- Lift your tongue tip to your alveolar ridge. The sides of the tongue will be lifted too.
- Pull your tongue tip away from the alveolar ridge just a little bit.
- Round your lips.
- Release air down your tongue and straight out your mouth.
- Your voice will be off.

PEACHIE SPEECHIE'S

Speech Sound Handbook

/ʃ/ Word List

Initial

1 Syllable

Shack
Shade
Shake
Shape
Share
Shark
Sharp
Shave
She
Shed
Sheep
Sheet
Shelf
Shin
Shine
Ship
Shock
Shoe
Shop
Short
Should
Shout
Shove
Show
Shut
Shy
Sure

2 Syllables

Shadow
Shaking
Shallow
Shampoo
Shamrock
Shaping
Sharing
Sharpen
Shattered
Shaving
Shelter
Sherbet
Shingles
Shiping
Shiver
Shocking
Shoelace
Shopping
Shortcake
Shower
Sugar

3 Syllables

Chandelier
Chaperone
Chicago
Shadowbox
Shampooing
Sharpener
Shivering
Shoemaker
Shortening

Medial

Action
Addition
Adoption
Bushes
Cashier
Caution
Collection
Cushion
Dashing
Dishes
Emotion
Extinction
Eyelashes
Fishing
Finishes
Flashcard
Flashlight
Horseshoe
Lotion
Mansion
Mission
Nation
Nashville
Nutrition
Ocean
Pressure
Push-ups
Pushes
Rushing
Seashore
Social
Special
Station
Sunshine
Tissue
Toothbrushes
Washcloth
Washing
Wishes

Final

Ash
Brush
Bush
Cash
Crash
Dash
Dish
English
Eyelash
Finish
Fish
Flash
Fresh
Gosh
Goldfish
Hush
Josh
Mash
Mustache
Paintbrush
Publish
Push
Rash
Selfish
Smash
Spanish
Starfish
Squish
Trash
Wash
Wish

Challenge

Multiple positions within the word

Shush
Sheepish
Shellfish
Shoeshine
Shoe brush
Shoeshop
Sheep shearing
Ship-to-shore
Shaving brush
Trash masher

PEACHIE SPEECHIE'S

Speech Sound Handbook

Eliciting /ʃ/

SH is a voiceless palato-alveolar fricative. The sides of the tongue lift to touch the upper molars. The blade of the tongue lifts also, almost touching the alveolar ridge. Lips are typically rounded. Air flows down the midline groove in the tongue to make the /sh/ sound. Children have typically mastered this sound by age 4.

Eliciting SH

- Teach basic anatomy of the mouth using a mouth model, visuals, and/or your own mouth with a mirror. Focus on the alveolar ridge, lateral margins of the tongue, and tip/blade of tongue for SH.
- Give step-by-step placement instructions.
  1. **Lift your tongue tip to touch your alveolar ridge.**
  2. **Make sure the back sides of your tongue are lifted up to touch your upper teeth.**
  3. **Pull your tongue tip back a little, away from the alveolar ridge.**
  4. **Round your lips.**
  5. **Blow air forward, sending it down the tongue and straight out the mouth.**
- Help them visualize the midline groove by telling the child to make a "bowl shape" with their tongue and blow air through the bowl.
- Rename the SH sound. You can call it the quiet sound ("Shhh baby is sleeping!") or the ocean sound (the sound of the waves) as you instruct them on placement.
- Hold your finger up to your lips as if you're telling someone to be quiet. Model the /ʃ/ sound and as you do, move your finger forward to show the forward air stream.
- Have the child sustain a whispered /i/ sound and then instruct them to round their lips and pull the tongue back slightly to achieve the /ʃ/ sound. You may also need to instruct them to close their jaw a bit.
- Shape from the ER sound. Instruct the child to say a whispered /ɝ/ and then round their lips and close their teeth so they are almost touching. The whispered /ɝ/ will turn into the /ʃ/ sound.
- Shape from the S sound. Instruct the child to sustain the /s/ sound and then pull their tongue tip back while rounding their lips to achieve the /ʃ/ sound.
- Say, "HUSH". Tell the child to sustain the /h/ sound. Then, instruct them to round their lips, close their jaw, and lift the tongue to achieve the /ʃ/. This may sound like they are slowly saying the word, "hush".
- Rub the upper lateral margins of the tongue with a lollipop, dental swab, or tongue depressor to increase awareness. Instruct them to lift the tongue so the sides touch the upper teeth. Then, instruct them to round their lips and blow out air for /ʃ/.
- Say this little chant to remember placement for SH. Lyrics: Sides up, tip back, lips round, Shhh. Scan the QR code for the video of this chant.

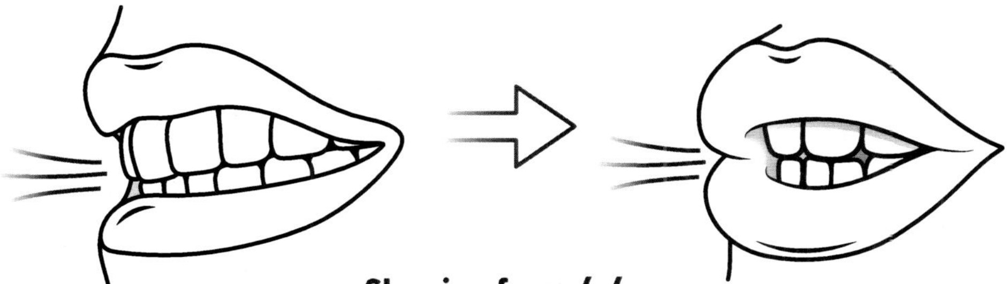

Shaping from /s/

Scan this QR code to go directly to our free video

SCAN ME

PEACHIE SPEECHIE'S

Speech Sound Handbook

The ZH Sound

/ʒ/

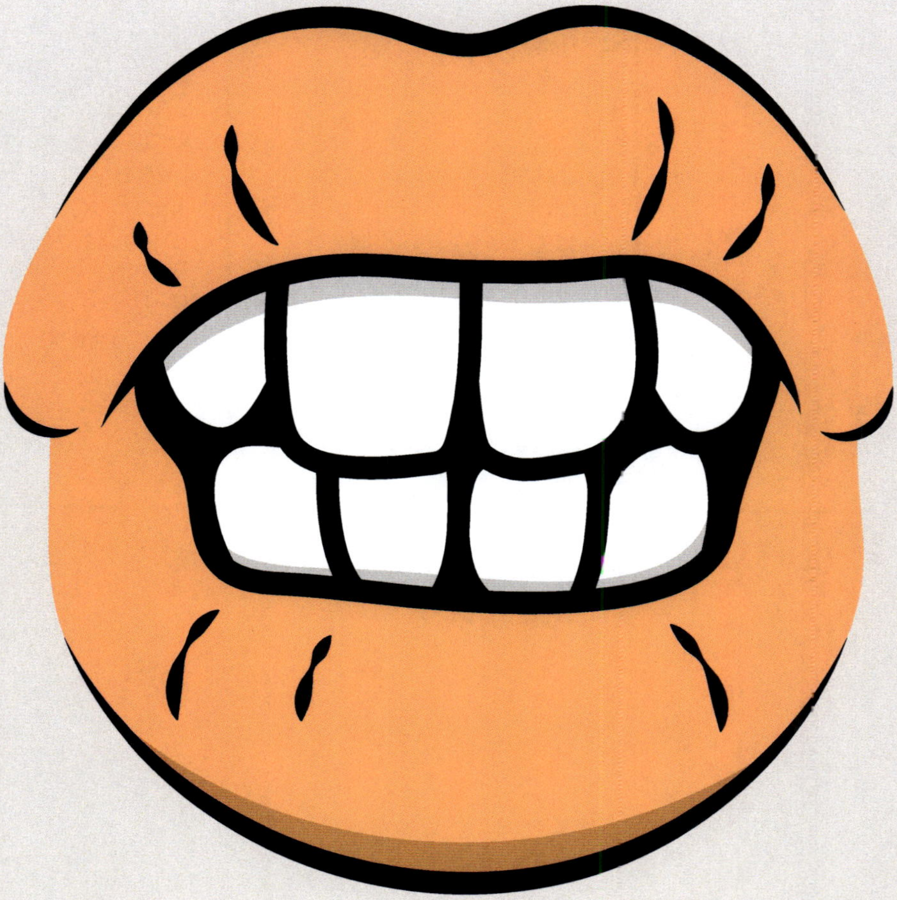

How to Say the ZH Sound

- Lift your tongue tip your alveolar ridge. The sides of the tongue will be lifted too.
- Pull your tongue tip away from the alveolar ridge just a little bit.
- Round your lips.
- Release air down your tongue and straight out your mouth.
- Your voice will be on.

PEACHIE SPEECHIE'S

Speech Sound Handbook

/ʒ/ Word List

Medial

2 Syllables

- Asia
- Closure
- Fusion
- Measure
- Pleasure
- Seizure
- Treasure
- Version
- Vision

3 Syllables

- Abrasion
- Casual
- Caucasian
- Conclusion
- Confusion
- Decision
- Division
- Erosion
- Explosion
- Invasion
- Inclusion
- Leisurely
- Measuring
- Persuasion
- Protrusion
- Seclusion
- Treasurer
- Usual
- Visual

Final

- Beige
- Camouflage
- Concierge
- Collage
- Corsage
- Decoupage
- Entourage
- Garage
- Luge
- Massage
- Mirage
- Prestige
- Rouge
- Sabotage

Eliciting /ʒ/

ZH is a voiced palato-alveolar fricative. The sides of the tongue lift to touch the upper molars. The blade of the tongue lifts also, almost touching the alveolar ridge. Lips are typically rounded. Air flows down the midline groove in the tongue to make the /ʒ/ sound. /ʒ/ is the voiced cognate of /ʃ/. Children have typically mastered this sound by age 5.

Eliciting ZH

- Teach basic anatomy of the mouth using a mouth model, visuals, and/or your own mouth with a mirror. Focus on the alveolar ridge, lateral margins of the tongue, and tip/blade of tongue for /ʒ/.
- Give step-by-step placement instructions.
    1. **Lift the tongue tip to touch your alveolar ridge.**
    2. **Make sure the back sides of your tongue are lifted up too. They will touch the upper teeth.**
    3. **Now pull your tongue tip back a little, away from the alveolar ridge.**
    4. **Round your lips.**
    5. **Blow voiced air forward, sending it down the tongue and straight out the mouth.**
- If the child can say the /ʃ/ sound, tell them to make a "noisy SH" by turning their voice on. You can place their hand on your throat as you say /ʃ/ and /ʒ/ to draw attention to voicing.
- Help them visualize the midline groove by telling the child to make a "bowl shape" with their tongue and blow air through the bowl with their voice turned on.
- Rename the /ʒ/ sound. You can call it the machine sound or the buzzy bowl sound as you instruct them on placement.
- Have the child sustain an /i/ sound and then instruct them to round their lips and pull the tongue back slightly to achieve the /ʒ/ sound. You may also need to instruct them to close their jaw a bit.
- Shape from the ER sound. Instruct the child to say /ɝ/ and then round their lips and close their teeth so they are almost touching. You may need to prompt them to slide their tongue forward a little bit also. The /ɝ/ will turn into the /ʒ/ sound.
- Shape from the Z sound. Instruct the child to sustain the /z/ sound and then pull their tongue tip back while rounding their lips to achieve the /ʃ/ sound.
- Rub the upper lateral margins of the tongue with a lollipop, dental swab, or tongue depressor to increase awareness. Instruct them to lift the tongue so the sides touch the upper teeth. Then, instruct them to round their lips and blow out voiced air for ZH.

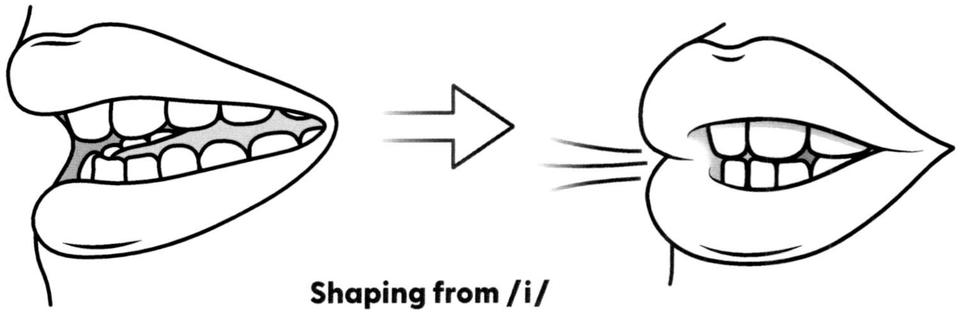

Shaping from /i/

PEACHIE SPEECHIE'S

Speech Sound Handbook

The H Sound

/h/

How to Say the H Sound

- Open your mouth a little bit.
- Push air forward out of your mouth.

PEACHIE SPEECHIE'S

Speech Sound Handbook

/h/ Word List

Initial

1 Syllable

Had, Hair, Half, Hall, Ham, Hand, Hang, Hard, Has, Hat, Haunt, He, Head, Health, Heart, Heat, Heel, Hen, Her, Here, Hi, Hid, Hike, Hill, Hint, Hip, His, Hiss, Hit, Hold, Home, Honk, Hoof, Hook, Hoop, Hop, Hope, Horse, Hot, House, How, Hug, Hulk, Hung, Hurt, Hush, Who, Whole, Whose

2 Syllables

Habit, Hair-do, Haiti, Hallway, Hammer, Hamper, Hamster, Handbag, Hanger, Happy, Harmful, Hatchet, Hazard, Headache, Headset, Healthy, Hearing, Hello, Hockey, Homeroom, Honey, Hornet, Hotdog, Hotel, Hurry, Hyper

3 Syllables

Habitat, Halloween, Hamburger, Handkerchief, Handlebar, Handwriting, Hanukkah, Happiness, Harmonize, Helium, Holiday, Homecoming, Honeybee, Horizon, However, Hurricane, Hydrogen, Hypnotize, Whoever

Medial

Aha, Ahead, Ahoy, Beehive, Behave, Birdhouse, Boohoo, Doghouse, Forehead, Grasshopper, Groundhog, Inhale, Keyhole, Ohio, Playhouse, Reheat, Rehearsal, Seahorse, Treehouse, Unhappy, Uphill, Yahoo

Challenge

Multiple positions within the word

Hedge hog, Half-and-half, Hula hoop

PEACHIE SPEECHIE'S

Speech Sound Handbook

Eliciting /h/

H is a voiceless glottal fricative. Air passes through the vocal folds, producing friction and creating the /h/ sound. Children have typically mastered this sound by age 3.

Eliciting H

- Tell the child to take a breath in, open their mouth a little bit, and send the air straight out to produce the /h/ sound.

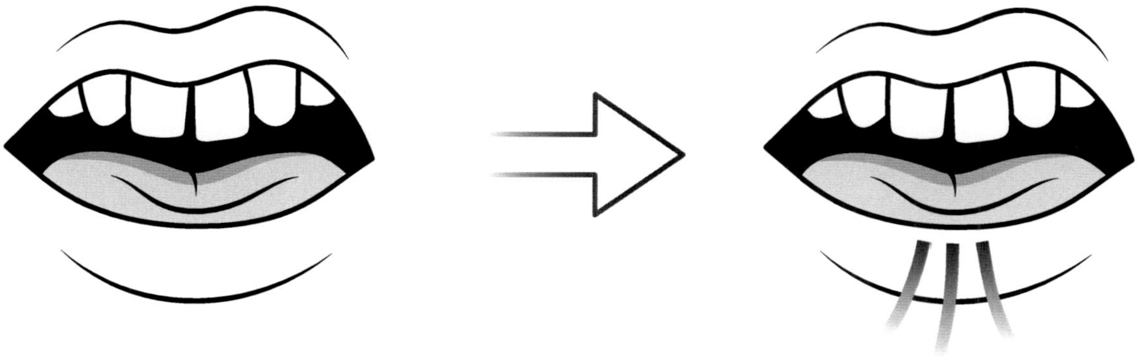

Open mouth **Let air out**

- Hold a small hand mirror up to the child's mouth and tell them to use enough air to fog up the mirror.
- Point to your throat as a reminder to the child to let air flow straight out through their glottis.
- Point to your mouth and then pull your finger out away from your mouth as you say the /h/ sound. This motion will remind them to sustain the sound, letting the airstream flow out.
- Pretend to laugh with force, "HA-HA-HA", and ask the child to imitate.
- Instruct the child to place their hand on their abdomen as they say, "Ha". Tell them to make it strong by using their abdominal muscles.
- Say, "ah-HA!" You can start by sustaining /a/ and then instruct them to push out a burst of air for /ha/.
- Rename H. You can call it the panting sound or the hot sound as you practice.
- Tell them to think about a dog panting, saying ha-ha-ha. Scan the QR code for an instructional video for /h/ featuring a panting dog.

Scan this QR code to go directly to our free video

SCAN ME

The CH Sound

/ʧ/

How to Say the CH Sound

- Lift your tongue up behind your alveolar ridge.
- Lift the back sides of you tongue up so they touch your molars.
- Round your lips.
- Press your tongue tip up and release a quick burst of air.

/ʧ/ Word List

Initial

1 Syllable

Chain
Chair
Chalk
Champ
Change
Chap
Charge
Charm
Chart
Chase
Chat
Cheat
Check
Cheer
Cheese
Chess
Chest
Chew
Chick
Chief
Child
Chill
Chin
Chips
Choice
Choke
Choose
Chug

2 Syllables

Cello
Challenge
Changing
Channel
Chapter
Charcoal
Charlie
Charming
Chatter
Checkers
Cheerful
Cheesecake
Cheetah
Cherry
Chicken
Children
Chilly
China
Chopsticks
Chosen
Chubby
Chutney

3 Syllables

Challenger
Champion
Charity
Chatterbox
Cheerleaders
Chewing gum
Chimpanzee

Medial

Achieve
Armchair
Beachball
Branches
Catcher
Coaches
Creature
Culture
Exchange
Future
Gesture
Hatchet
Inches
Ketchup
Keychain
Kitchen
Lunches
Matches
Nachos
Nature
Peachy
Picture
Question
Richest
Statue
Teacher
Touching
Vulture
Watchful
Witches

Final

Attach
Beach
Bench
Brunch
Catch
Coach
Crunch
Each
Fetch
French
Grouch
Hopscotch
Much
Ouch
Ostrich
Peach
Punch
Reach
Rich
Scratch
Speech
Such
Teach
Touch
Watch
Which

Challenge

Multiple positions within the word

Cha-Cha
Chit chat
Chinchilla
Chow chow
Church

Eliciting /ʧ/

CH is a voiceless palato-alveolar affricate. The tip of the tongue contacts the post-alveolar ridge while the back lateral margins of the tongue lift as well, touching the back molars. The lips are rounded. Air pressure builds as the tongue tip presses against the post-alveolar ridge and quickly releases a quick burst of air, the /ʧ/ sound. Children have typically mastered this sound by age 4.

Eliciting CH

- Use a mouth model, visual illustrations, or your own mouth to teach anatomy, focusing on the alveolar ridge, tongue tip, blade, and upper molars for the CH sound.
- Make a tongue out of play dough and use with a plastic or paper mouth model to show how it should be positioned with the tongue tip lifted up just behind the alveolar ridge.
- Give step-by-step placement instructions.
    1. **Lift your tongue tip up behind your alveolar ridge.**
    2. **The back sides of your tongue will be touching the back molars.**
    3. **Round your lips.**
    4. **Release a quick burst of air. As the air pressure is released, your tongue tip will press against the roof of your mouth and then drop a little.**

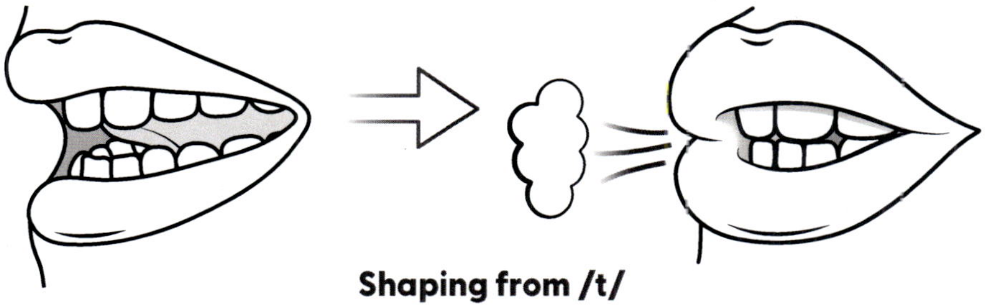

Shaping from /t/

- Rub the alveolar ridge and tongue tip/blade with a lollipop or dental swab to increase awareness of articulators.
- Shape from the T sound. Instruct the child to say the /t/ sound with their tongue tip on their alveolar ridge. Then, tell them to round their lips, saying /t/ with their lips round. Last, tell them to keep their lips round, and pull their tongue tip back a little bit and say /t/ again. It should sound like the /ʧ/ sound.
- Tell them to say the /t/ sound and the /ʃ/ sound at the same time. Model it for them and ask them to repeat. This can sometimes result in a /ʧ/ sound.
- Shape from the SH sound. Instruct the child to sustain the /ʃ/ sound and then stop the airflow by lifting their tongue tip as if they are preparing to say the /t/ sound. Then, repeat that again but this time as they lift their tongue tip up, tell them to push out air again, keeping their lips round and voice off. This will sound like SH → T → CH.
- Rename the CH sound. You can call it the sneeze sound and practice saying Achoo!
- Water Bottle Visual. The /ʧ/ sound is made with a quick burst of hair. Use a spray water bottle filled with water and puff out bursts of air with it as a visual for the child. You can also talk about water running out of a faucet being like the SH sound vs. water puffing out of a water bottle being like the CH sound.
- If they are having difficulty with lip rounding, you can place your index finger and thumb on the corners of the child's mouth to gently encourage lip rounding/protrusion.
- Say this little chant to remember placement for CH. Lyrics: Tongue up, Lips Round, Burst of Air - CH! Scan the QR code for the video of this chant.

SCAN ME

Scan this QR code to go directly to our free video

The J Sound

/ʤ/

How to Say the J Sound

- Lift your tongue tip up behind your alveolar ridge.
- Lift the back sides of your tongue up so they touch your molars.
- Round your lips.
- Press your tongue tip up and release a quick burst of voiced air.

PEACHIE SPEECHIE'S

Speech Sound Handbook

/dʒ/ Word List

Initial

1 Syllable

Gem
Germ
Gym
Jam
Jar
Jaws
Jay
Jazz
Jeans
Jeep
Jet
Jew
Job
Join
Joke
Joy
Judge
Jug
Juice
Jump
June
Junk
Just

2 Syllables

Gentle
Gerbil
Giant
Giraffe
Gypsy
Jacket
Jaguar
Japan
Jealous
Jello
Jelly
Jewel
Jiggle
Jockey
Jogging
Jolly
Journal
Joyful
Juicy
July
Junior
Jury

3 Syllables

General
Germany
Jellybean
Jellyfish
Jeopardy
Journalist
Jupiter
Justify

Medial

Adjectives
Adjust
Ageless
Agent
Angel
Badger
Cages
Detergent
Digest
Dodgeball
Edges
Engineer
Egypt
Fidget
Fragile
Graduate
Hedgehog
Legend
Magic
Magician
Margarine
Object
Oranges
Pages
Pajamas
Pigeon
Pledging
Region
Rigid
Soldier
Subject
Suggest
Surgeon
Tragic
Urgent
Vegetables
Wages

Final

Age
Avenge
Badge
Bandage
Cabbage
Cage
College
Damage
Dodge
Edge
Fudge
Garbage
Huge
Image
Knowledge
Language
Ledge
Manage
Marriage
Package
Page
Postage
Sausage
Smudge
Stage
Storage
Teenage
Village
Voyage
Wedge

Challenge

Multiple positions within the word

Judges
Jumping jacks
Geology
Ginger
Gingerbread
Gingivitis
Hodgepodge

Eliciting /dʒ/

J is a voiced palato-alveolar affricate. The tip of the tongue contacts the post-alveolar ridge while the back lateral margins of the tongue lift as well, touching the back molars. The lips are rounded. Air pressure builds as the tongue tip presses against the post-alveolar ridge and quickly releases a quick burst of voiced air, the /dʒ/ sound. Children have typically mastered this sound by age 4.

Eliciting J

- Use a mouth model, visual illustrations, or your own mouth to teach anatomy, focusing on the alveolar ridge, tongue tip, blade, and upper molars for the J sound.
- Make a tongue out of play dough and use it with a plastic or paper mouth model to show how it should be positioned with the tongue tip lifted up just behind the alveolar ridge.
- Give step-by-step placement instructions.
    1. **Lift your tongue tip up behind your alveolar ridge.**
    2. **The back sides of your tongue will be touching the back molars.**
    3. **Round your lips.**
    4. **Release a quick burst of voiced air. As the air pressure is released, your tongue tip will press against the roof of your mouth and then drop a little.**
- Rub the alveolar ridge and tongue tip/blade with a lollipop or dental swab to increase awareness of articulators.
- Shape from the D sound. Instruct the child to say the /d/ sound with their tongue tip on their alveolar ridge. Then, tell them to round their lips, saying /d/ with their lips round. Last, tell them to keep their lips round, and pull their tongue tip back a little bit and say /d/ again. It should sound like the /dʒ/ sound.

- Tell them to say the /d/ sound and the /ʒ/ sound at the same time. Model it for them and ask them to repeat. This can sometimes result in a /dʒ/ sound.
- Shape from the /ʒ/ sound. Instruct the child to sustain the /ʒ/ sound and then stop the airflow by lifting their tongue tip as if they are preparing to say the /d/ sound. Then, repeat that again but this time as they lift their tongue tip up, tell them to push out air again, keeping their lips round and voice off. This will sound like /ʒ/→/d/→/dʒ/.
- Shape from the /i/ sound. Instruct the child to sustain /i/ and then round their lips as they continue to say /i/. Next, ask them to tap their tongue tip/blade up to their alveolar ridge and release the noisy burst. This may result in an accurate /dʒ/.
- Rename the J sound. You can call it the jumping jacks sound or the jingle bell sound as you practice.
- Instruct the child to place their hand on your throat as you produce both the /ʃ/ and the /dʒ/ sounds to draw attention to the voicing required for /dʒ/
- If they are having difficulty with lip rounding, you can place your index finger and thumb on the corners of the child's mouth to gently encourage lip rounding/protrusion.
- Say this little chant to remember placement for J. Lyrics: Tongue up, Lips round, Noisy burst, J! Scan the QR code for the video of this chant.

Scan this QR code to go directly to our free video

SCAN ME

PEACHIE SPEECHIE'S

Speech Sound Handbook

The M Sound

/ m /

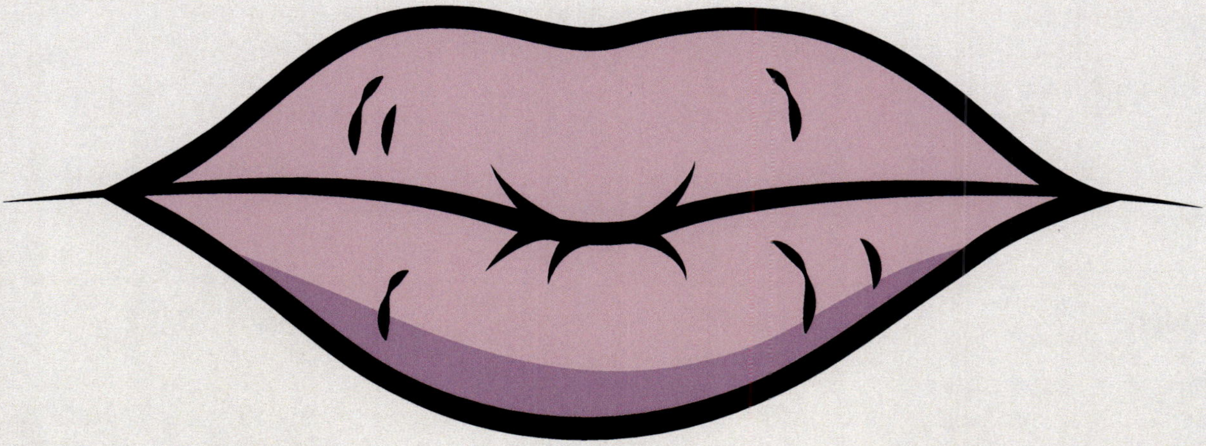

How to Say the M Sound

- Put your lips together and keep them together as you turn your voice on.
- The air will pass through your nose.

/m/ Word List

Initial

1 Syllable

Ma
Mad
Made
Mail
Main
Make
Mall
Man
Map
March
Mark
Marry
Mask
Math
May
Me
Meal
Mean
Meet
Mess
Mice
Might
Milk
Mint
Miss
Month
Moose
Mop
More
Move
Much
My

2 Syllables

Machine
Magnet
Major
Manners
Many
Market
Marriage
Mascot
Master
Measured
Medal
Menu
Merry
Mickey
Middle
Mirror
Mitten
Model
Monday
Monkey
Monster
Mother
Movie
Moving
Muffin
Muscle
Mustard
Myself

3 Syllables

Magazine
Magician
Manager
Mannequin
Manual
Measuring
Meredith
Mexico
Microphone
Microwave
Millionaire
Missouri
Montana
Musical

Medial

Aiming
Almost
Amount
Camel
Chimney
Climate
Comet
Coming
Common
Damage
Dreaming
Drummer
Emma
Famous
Grammar
Hammer
Himself
Human
Image
Lemon
Rumor
Swimming
Someone
Summer
Timer
Timmy
Woman

Final

Aim
Am
Boom
Bum
Calm
Climb
Comb
Dime
Doom
Drum
From
Game
Gum
Gym
Ham
Him
Home
Hum
I'm
Jam
Lamb
Name
Palm
Prime
Rhyme
Same
Slime
Some
Steam
Swim
Team
Them
Thumb
Time
Zoom

Challenge

Multiple positions within the word

Mama
Mommy
Mailman
Mailwoman
Mammal
Mammoth
Marshmallow
Miami
Medium
Member
Membrane
Mermaid
Monument
Motor home
Mummy
Mushroom

Eliciting /m/

M is a voiced bilabial nasal sound. The lips come together as the velum lowers and air comes out the nasal cavity. Children have typically mastered this sound by age 3.

Eliciting M

- Model the /m/ sound to the child. Emphasize bringing your lips together.
- Use illustrated visuals to show how air will flow through the nasal cavity.
- Give step-by-step placement instructions.
    1. Put your lips together and take a breath in through your nose.
    2. Keep your lips together and let the air come out your nose as your voice turns on for /m/.

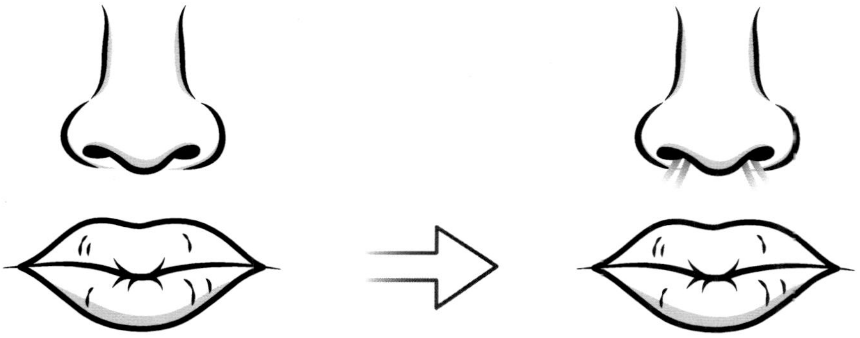

Close your lips

Sound comes out your nose

- Rub the child's upper and lower lips with a lollipop or dental swab to draw attention to them. Then, ask them to put their lips together and practice /m/.
- Rename the M sound. You can call it the humming sound or the yummy sound as you say it with the child. Ask them to hum or pretend they ate something yummy.
- Ask the child to gently touch the sides of their nose to feel the vibration as they say the /m/ sound.
- Shape from the N sound. Have the child sustain /n/ and then instruct them to close their lips and drop their tongue down a bit to achieve the /m/ sound.
- Ask the child to sustain a vowel such as /a/ or /ʌ/. Place your index finger just under the child's lower lip and move it upward to meet the top lip as they hold the vowel. Prompt them to direct the air out their nose.
- Say this little chant about M being the "yummy sound". Lyrics: M is a yummy sound, Mmm, Mmm, Mmm! Scan the QR code for the video of this chant.

Scan this QR code to go directly to our free video

SCAN ME

The N Sound

/n/

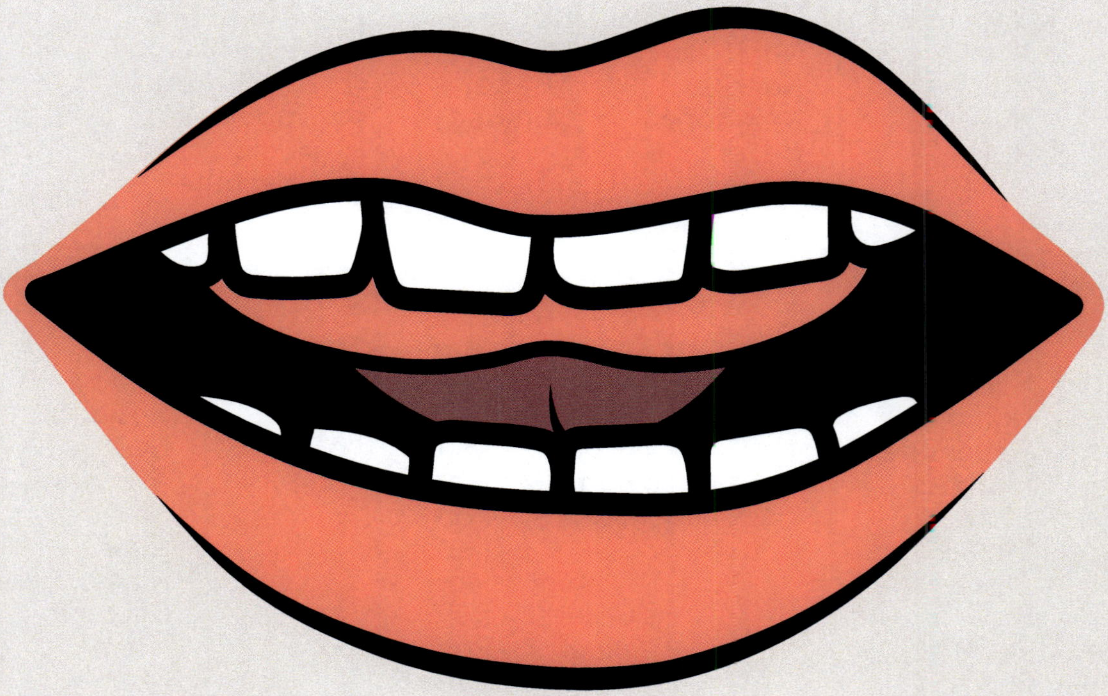

How to Say the N Sound

- Lift your tongue tip up to your alveolar ridge.
- Turn your voice on.
- The air will pass through your nose.

PEACHIE SPEECHIE'S

Speech Sound Handbook

/n/ Word List

Initial

1 Syllable

Gnome
Knee
Knife
Nail
Name
Neat
Neck
Need
Nest
New
Next
Nice
Night
No
Noise
North
Nose
Not
Note
Now
Numb
Nurse
Nut

2 Syllables

Knitting
Knowing
Knowledge
Nacho
Naked
Nation
Navy
Necklace
Needle
Neighbor
Never
Nickel
Ninja
Noisy
Noodle
Normal
Notebook
Nostril
Nothing
Novel
Nugget
Number

3 Syllables

Natural
Nausea
Nautical
Nebraska
Negative
Neighborhood
Networking
Nevada
Newspaper
Nobody
Nucleus
November
Nursery
Nutcracker

Medial

Anna
Any
Animal
Banner
Bonus
Bunny
Canal
Cannot
Canoe
Chimney
China
Cleanup
Denim
Dinner
Dinosaur
Donut
Final
Finish
Funny
Hanukkah
Honey
Honor
Lightning
Lemonade
Manners
Many
Money
Owner
Panic
Peanut
Penny
Pineapple
Planet
Pony
Rainbow
Runner
Sooner
Sunny
Tennis
Tiny
Universe
Venus
Volcano
Winner

Final

An
Been
Bone
Brain
Bun
Can
Chin
Clown
Coin
Dine
Down
Fan
Fun
Gain
Gone
Green
Hen
In
Lane
Line
Man
Mean
Mine
Moon
One
Pan
Pen
Plane
Rain
Ran
Seen
Sign
Skin
Spoon
Stone
Sun
Ten
Then
Than
Town
Train
Van
When
Yawn
Zone

Challenge

Multiple positions within the word

Nancy
National
Neon
Nectarine
Nina
Nine
Ninety-Nine
Nitrogen
Noon
Noun
Nun
Nutrition
Banana
Cinnamon
Knick nack
Nickname

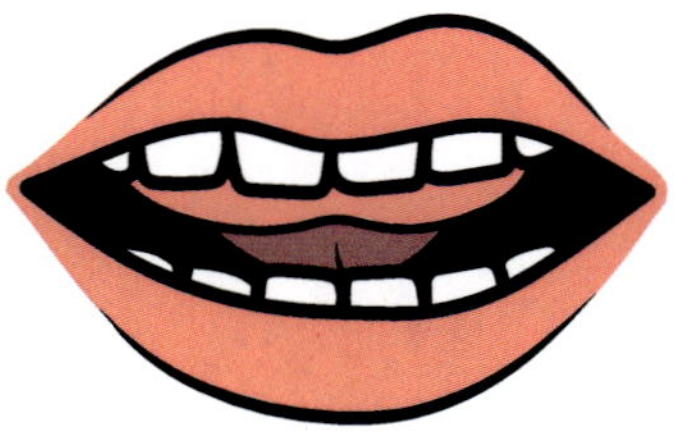

Eliciting /n/

N is a voiced lingua-alveolar nasal sound. The tongue tip lifts to touch the alveolar ridge. The lateral margins of the tongue are also lifted, touching the upper teeth. The velum is lowered and air escapes through the nasal cavity. Children have typically mastered this sound by age 3.

Eliciting N

- Use illustrated visuals to show how air will flow through the nasal cavity.
- Give step-by-step placement instructions.
    1. **Lift the tongue tip up to the alveolar ridge. The sides of the tongue will lift, too.**
    2. **Breathe in through your nose**
    3. **Turn on your voice, letting the sound and air come out your nose.**
- Gently touch the child's nose as they practice to remind them that air escapes from the nasal cavity for the /n/ sound.
- Rub the alveolar ridge with a lollipop or tongue depressor to draw awareness to the spot they need to place their tongue.
- Use the tip of a tongue depressor to gently elevate the tongue tip, directing it to the alveolar ridge.
- Hold a small compact hand mirror directly under the child's nostrils as they practice to encourage airflow through the nasal cavity. Tell them you want to see fog on the mirror.
- Instruct the child to place their index finger across their upper lip. Tell them to feel for the air coming out of their nose when they produce the /n/ sound.
- Rename the N sound. You can call it the nose sound or the gnat sound as you practice.
- Shape from the /m/ sound. Instruct the child to hold out /m/ and then lift the tongue tip to the alveolar ridge. Then tell them to open their mouth just a little bit, to turn /m/ into /n/.
- Shape from /i/. Ask the child to sustain the /i/ sound and then bring the tongue tip up to the alveolar ridge. Point to their nose as a reminder of nasal airflow.
- Song to help remember placement for /n/. Lyrics: Tongue goes up, Air through your nose, That's the way the N sound goes! Scan the QR code for the video of this song.

Scan this QR code to go directly to our free video

SCAN ME

PEACHIE SPEECHIE'S

Speech Sound Handbook

The NG Sound

/ŋ/

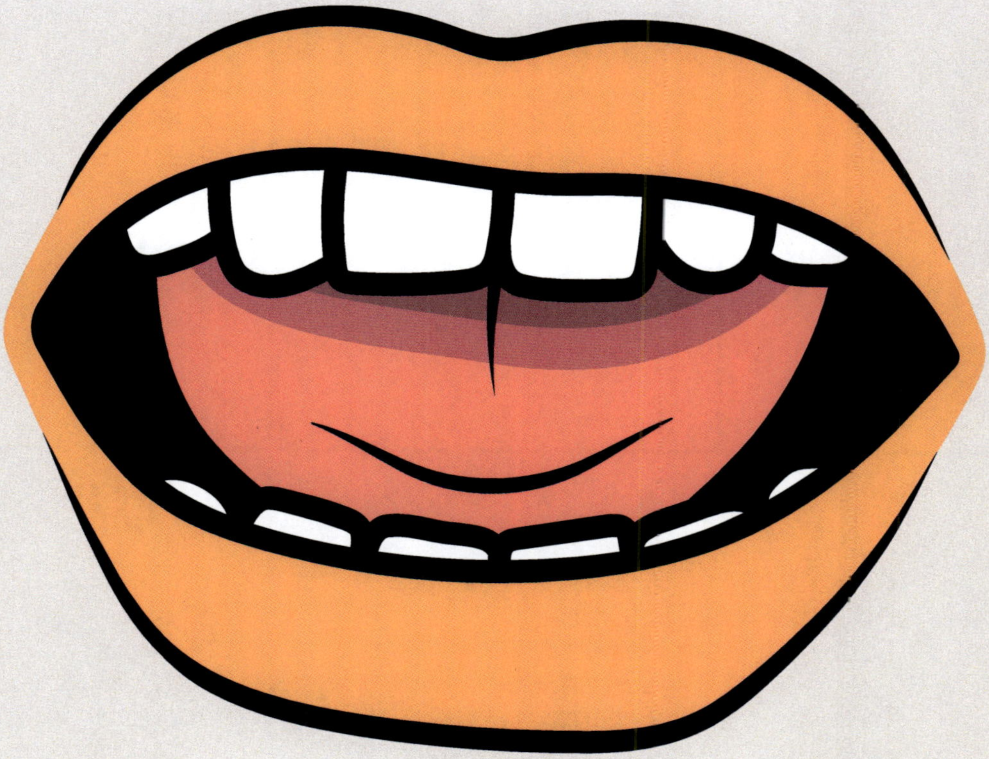

How to Say the NG Sound

- **Lift the back of your tongue to your soft palate.**
- **A voiced airstream will pass through your nose.**

PEACHIE SPEECHIE'S

Speech Sound Handbook

/ŋ/ Word List

Medial

2 Syllables

Anger
Bongo
Finger
Fungus
Hanger
Hungry
Jingle
Jungle
Kingdom
Longer
Singer
Stronger
Tango
Tingle
Wrangler
Youngest

3 Syllables

Angora
Buckingham
Bungalow
Chewing gum
Elongate
Fingernail
Fingerpaint
Flamingo
Hearing aid
Kangaroo
Marching band
Singapore
Washington

Final

1 Syllable

Bang
Bring
Cling
Fang
Hang
King
Long
Lung
Rang
Ring
Sing
Song
Spring
Sting
Strong
Swing
Thing
Tongue
Wing
Wrong

Final

2 Syllables

Asking
Baking
Bedding
Bending
Boating
Bowling
Buying
Buzzing
Camping
Caring
Catching
Charming
Climbing
Coming
Cycling
Dining
Doing
Driving
Eating
Evening
Falling
Feeding
Feeling
Finding
Going
Guessing
Having
Jogging
Laughing
Leading
Looking
Making
Morning
Standing
Swimming
Talking
Throwing
Waiting
Walking
Working

Challenge

Multiple positions within the word

Angling
Banging
Belonging
Hong Kong
Ping Pong
Ding Dong
Lingering

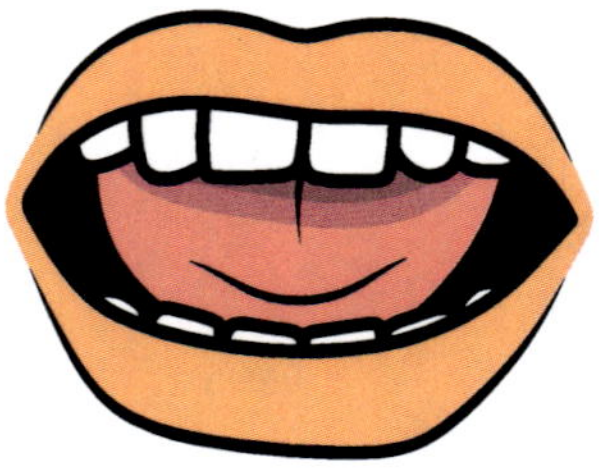

PEACHIE SPEECHIE'S

Speech Sound Handbook

Eliciting /ŋ/

NG is a voiced velar nasal sound. The back of the tongue lifts to the velum. The back sides of the tongue touch the back molars and inner gum line. The velum lowers and a voiced airstream is released through the nasal cavity to produce /ŋ/. Children have typically mastered this sound by age 3.

Eliciting NG

- Use a mouth model or visuals to discuss anatomy, focusing on the back of the tongue and velum for the /ŋ/ sound.
- Use an anatomy diagram/illustrated visuals to show airflow through the nasal cavity.
- Use a mouth model and a plastic tongue, tongue made out of play-dough, or your hand, to demonstrate elevation of the back of the tongue up to the velum.
- Give step-by-step placement instructions.
    1. **Lift the back of your tongue up to your velum (the velum will be in a lowered position).**
    2. **Turn on your voice and send the air out of your nose.**
- Rub the velum and back of tongue with a lollipop or dental swab to increase awareness of the articulators involved in production of the /ŋ/ sound.
- Gently place your thumb and index finger on the child's neck under the chin as a reminder to lift the back of the tongue.
- If they are able to say /k/ or /g/, you can tell them to "get their tongue ready" in the /k/ or /g/ position and then direct air out through their nose.
- Hold a small compact mirror under the child's nose as they practice the /ŋ/ sound to emphasize air escaping through the nasal cavity.
- Instruct the child to place their index finger on the side of their nose to feel the vibration as /ŋ/ is produced.
- Shape from the /i/ sound. Ask the child to sustain /i/, which encourages elevation of the lateral tongue margins. Then, instruct them to elevate the back of the tongue to the velum as they direct air out their nose.
- Rename the /ŋ/ sound. You can call it the ding ding bell sound or the ringing gong sound as you practice.

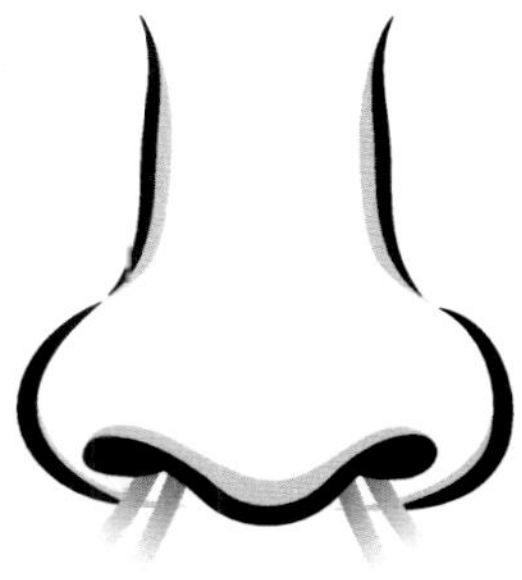

PEACHIE SPEECHIE'S

Speech Sound Handbook

The W Sound

/w/

How to Say the W Sound

- Round your lips and pull your tongue up and back as you make the sound.
- Your voice will be on.

W is called a "glide" because your tongue glides into a new position.

/w/ Word List

Initial *1 Syllable*

Wag
Wait
Wake
Walk
Wall
Wand
Want
Warm
Was
Wash
Waste
Watch
Wave
Way
We
We'll
We're
Wear
Web
Weight
Weird
Well
Were
West
Wide
Wife
Will
Wing
Wipe
Wish
With
Won
Wood
Work
World

2 Syllables

Oneself
Waffle
Wagging
Wagon
Waited
Wallet
Walnut
Walrus
Wander
Wanting
Wishing
Water
Wavy
Wearing
Weather
Wedding
Wiggle
Window
Winter
Wishing
Without
Wizard
Woman
Worker
Worry

3 Syllables

Wallpaper
Washington
Waterfall
Watering
Wintergreen
Wolverine
Wonderful
Woodpecker
Worrisome
Wyoming

Medial *2 Syllables*

Always
Awake
Away
Beware
Cobweb
Freeway
Goodwill
Hallway
Jaguar
Jewish
Kiwi
Midwest
Mouthwash
Pathway
Rewind
Sandwich
Seaweed
Someone

Medial *3 Syllables*

Awaken
Candlewax
Halloween
Handiwork
Hawaii
Microwave
Midwestern
Rainwater
Unaware

Phrases *3 Syllables*

Walking stick
Well mannered
Window box
Wisdom teeth
Witness stand

Challenge

Multiple positions within the word

Bow wow
Chihuahua
One way
Water wings
Wide awake
Wishy washy
Werewolf
Woodwork
Worldwide

Eliciting /w/

W is a voiced labial glide. The back of the tongue lifts to nearly touch the velum. The lips are rounded and the voice is on as air is directed out of the mouth through the rounded opening in the lips. Children have typically mastered this sound by age 3.

Eliciting W

- Point to your mouth as you model the sound, emphasizing the lip rounding required to produce /w/.
- Make a tongue out of play dough and use it to demonstrate how the back of the tongue elevates a bit for the /w/ sound.
- Give step-by-step placement instructions.
    1. Round your lips.
    2. Lift the back of the tongue up.
    3. Turn your voice on as you glide from /w/ into the next sound.
- Explain to the child that /w/ is a glide. This means that during production, the mouth is moving (gliding!) into the vowel following /w/. You can practice this movement during syllable drills (way, we, why, woah, woo).
- Shape from the /u/ sound. Tell the child to sustain the /u/ sound ("ooooo") and then instruct them to round their lips even more to make the /w/ sound. Then, they will release it into the /ə/ vowel. This will end up sounding like /uwə/ ("Ooo-wuh").

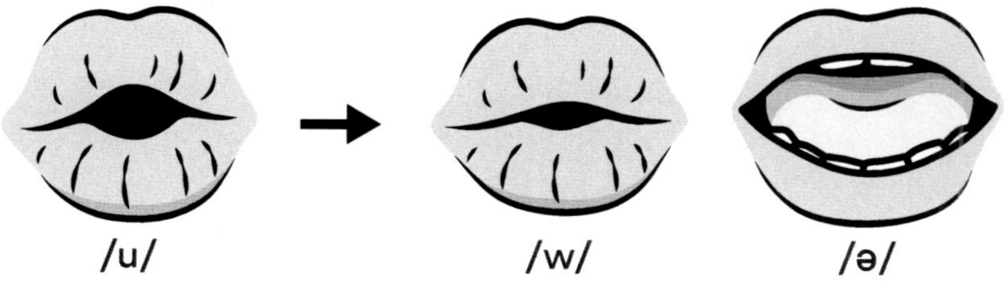

- Use your fingers to make a pinching motion on the outer edges of the lips, as pictured below. This is a visual cue to remind the child to round their lips.
- Song to help remember placement for /w/ Lyrics: Tongue's a little up, Lips are very round, That's the way you say your W sound! Scan the QR code for the video of this song.

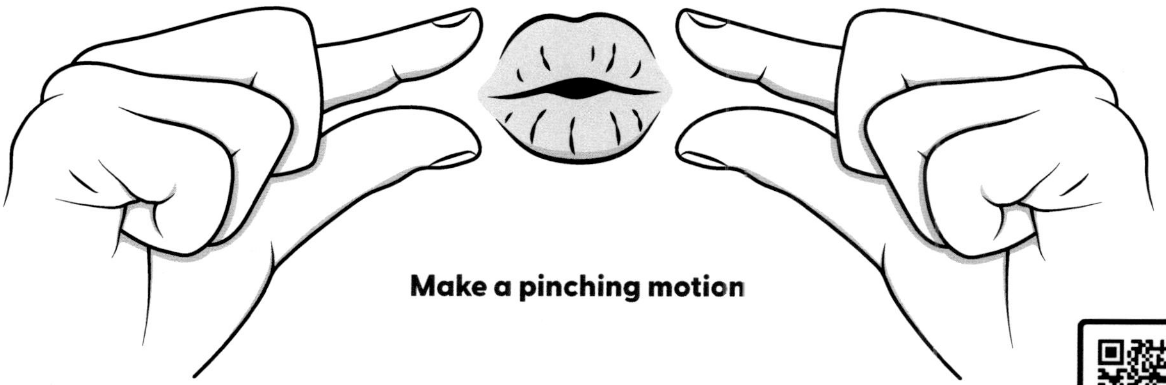

Scan this QR code to go directly to our free video

SCAN ME

The Y Sound

/j/

How to Say the Y Sound

- **Spread your lips into a slight smile.**
- **Lift up your tongue (like you're going to say "EE").**
- **Your voice will be on.**

Y is called a "glide" because your tongue glides into a new position.

PEACHIE SPEECHIE'S

Speech Sound Handbook

/j/ Word List

Initial

1 Syllable

Use
Yacht
Yak
Yam
Yank
Yap
Yard
Yea
Year
Yeast
Yell
Yes
Yet
Yolk
You
You'd
Your
Youth
Yum

2 Syllables

Unique
Unit
Usage
Useful
User
Utah
Yachting
Yahoo
Yardstick
Yearly
Yearning
Yelling
Yellow
Yeti
Yodel
Yoga
Yogurt
Younger
Youthful
Yummy

3 Syllables

Eureka
Unicorn
Uniform
United
Universe
Usual
Utensil
Youthfully

Medial

Australian
Bayou
Calculate
Canyon
Coyote
Crayon
Genius
Hawaiian
Kayak
Lawyer
Loyal
Mayan
Million
Monument
Papaya
Reuse
Royal
Savior
Senior
Tortilla
Value
Virginia

Blends

Beauty
Bugle
Cube
Cure
Few
Future
Fumes
Huge
Human
Mule
Music
Pupil
Viewer

Challenge

Multiple positions within the word

Uvula
Ying Yang
Yo-Yo

Eliciting /j/

Y is a voiced lingua-palatal glide. The tip and blade of the tongue elevate a bit. The lateral margins of the tongue elevate also, touching the inner teeth. The voice is on, as the tongue glides into position for the following vowel. The IPA symbol for the Y sound is /j/. Children have typically mastered this sound by age 3.

Eliciting Y

- The /j/ sound begins with the /i/ sound. Model this to the child by shining a light in your mouth as you say /i/ and then transition into the /j/ sound, so the child can see the tongue movement. This might sound like /ijə/, "Eeee-Yuh".

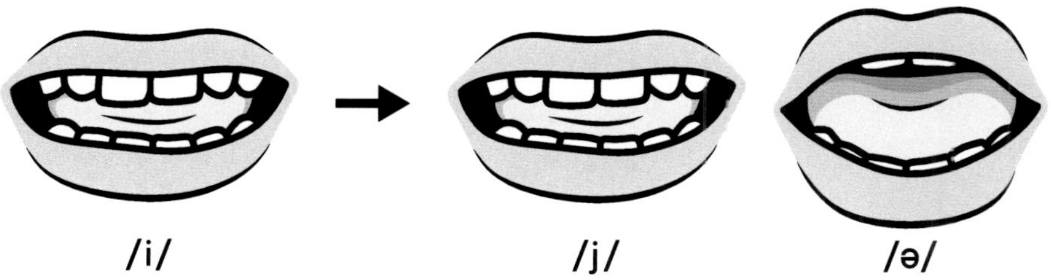

- Have the child sustain the /i/ sound and then gently lower their chin.
- Instruct the child to say /i/ and then /u/. Have them do this rapidly, and it will sound like they are saying the word "you".
- Explain to the child that /j/ is a glide. This means that during production, the mouth is moving (gliding!) into the vowel following /j/. You can practice this movement during syllable drills (yay, yee, yai, yo, you).
- Rub the lateral margins of the tongue with a lollipop and tell the child to lift the sides up so that they touch inside the upper teeth. You can also rub the blade of the tongue and tell them to lift it, but don't let it touch the roof of their mouth. This may help increase awareness of articulators and facilitate accurate production.
- Rename the /j/ sound. You can call it the cheering sound (Yay! Yay!) as you practice.

PEACHIE SPEECHIE'S

Speech Sound Handbook

The L Sound

/l/

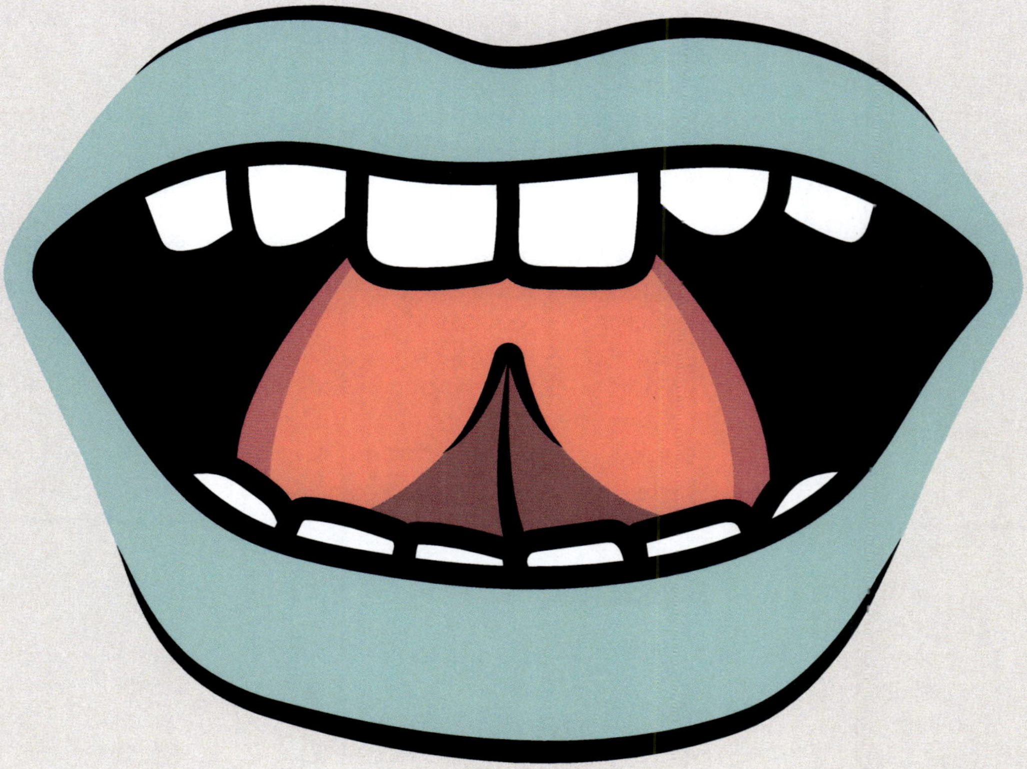

How to Say the L Sound

- Put your tongue tip behind your teeth on your alveolar ridge.
- Turn your voice on.

PEACHIE SPEECHIE'S

Speech Sound Handbook

/l/ Word List

Initial

1 Syllable

Laid
Lake
Lamb
Lamp
Land
Lap
Large
Lash
Late
Laugh
Lawn
Lead
Leaf
Leash
Leaves
Leg
Less
Lice
Lick
Lid
Life
Lift
Light
Like
Lime
Lip
List
Loaf
Lock
Long
Look
Lose
Lost
Loud
Love
Low
Lump
Lunch

2 Syllables

Lady
Landing
Language
Lantern
Larger
Laser
Later
Laughing
Laundry
Lava
Lawyer
Lazy
Leader
Leafy
Leather
Leaving
Legend
Lesson
Letter
Lettuce
License
Licking
Lighten
Limeade
Lion
Lipstick
Liquid
Listen
Liver
Living
Lizard
Llama
Lobster
Locker
London
Looking
Losing
Lower
Lucky
Lying

3 Syllables

Ladybug
Latitude
Lavender
Layering
Leadership
Legacy
Lemonade
Liberty
Library
Licorice
Lifesaver
Limerick
Limited
Litterbug
Location
Longitude
Lottery
Luckiest
Lumberjack

Medial

2 Syllables

Alarm
Alike
Alive
Allow
Alone
Balance
Ballet
Balloon
Belly
Belong
Below
Bowling
Bully
Ceiling
Cellar
Cello
Chili
Cola
College
Collect
Color
Dollar
Dolly
Elect
Eyelash
Fallen
Filling
Follow
Gallon
Halo
Hello
Highly
Jelly
July
Kelly
Mellow
Melon
Olive
Pillow
Pollute
Pulling
Really
Relax
Ruler
Sailor
Salad
Salon
Shallow
Silence
Smelling
Smiling
Solar
Stolen
Swallow
Talent
Talon
Toilet
Tulip
Value
Village
Volley
Wallet
Wally
Yelling
Yellow

Medial

3 Syllables

Allergic
Ambulance
Antelope
Balancing
Bologna
Broccoli
Buffalo
Calendar
Cantaloupe
Celebrate
Celery
Challenging
Collection
Colorful
Counselor
Delaware
Deliver
Electric
Elephant
Envelope
Family
Finalize
Follower
Galaxy
Gasoline
Gorilla
Halloween
Holiday
Italy
Marmalade
Marshmallow
Melody
Pelican
Policing
Relative
Skeleton
Solution
Syllabus
Televise
Valentine
Vanilla
Violet
Volunteer

Final

1 Syllable

Aisle
All
Ball
Bell
Bill
Bowl
Braille
Call
Cool
Crawl
Deal
Doll
Drool
Eel
Fail
Fall
Full
Girl
Goal
Hall
Heal
Hill
Mail
Meal
Nail
Oil
Owl
Peel
Pill
Pool
Quail
Real
Rule
Sail
School
Seal
She'll
Skill
Smell
Smile
Tail
Tell
Tool
Wall
Whale
Wheel
Whole
Will
Yell

2 Syllables

Anthill
Angel
Apple
Canal
Cancel
Control
Detail
Enroll
Equal
Exhale
Eyeball
Football
Hotel
Jewel
Joyfull
Kickball
Meanwhile
Meatball
Motel
Oatmeal
Oval
Pastel
Pencil
People
Pinwheel
Real
Reptile
Royal
Schedule
Scoopful
Seagull
Snowball
Symbol
Toenail
Towel
Until
Vowel

L-Blends and Challenge Word List

/bl/		/fl/		/gl/		/kl/	
Black	Blond	Flair	Flip	Glad	Gloomy	Clap	Climbed
Blast	Blouse	Flakes	Float	Glass	Glottis	Class	Closed
Bleed	Blowing	Flame	Floor	Glide	Glove	Claws	Cloth
Blink	Blue	Flag	Flower	Glitter	Glow	Clean	Clown
Blocks	Blurry	Flight	Fluffy	Globe	Glue	Cleats	Clue

/pl/		/sl/		Challenge *(Multiple placements)*		
Place	Play	Slap	Slim	Bluebell	Lonely	Volleyball
Plan	Please	Sleep	Slope	La La Land	Lemon-lime	
Plane	Plop	Sleeve	Slug	Lilly	Lullaby	
Plant	Plug	Sleigh	Slice	Lollipop	Sloppily	
Plate	Plus	Slide	Sly			

L-Blend Visual

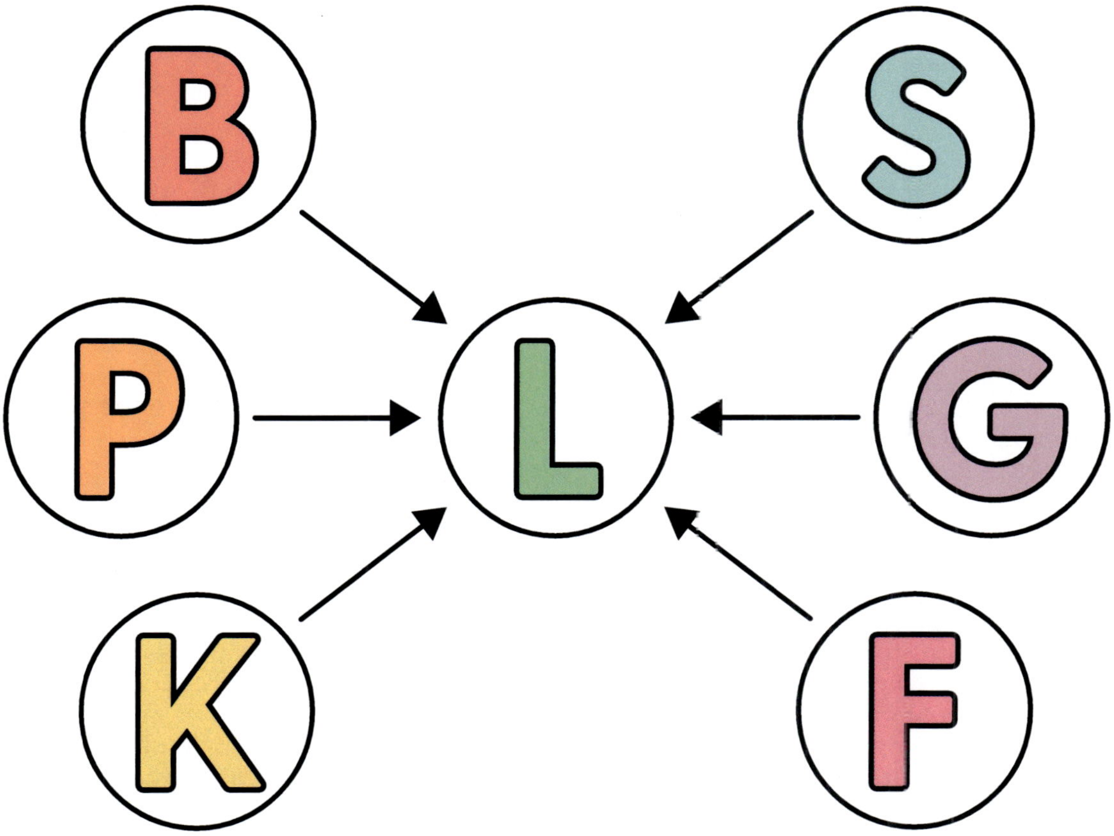

PEACHIE SPEECHIE'S

Speech Sound Handbook

Eliciting /l/

L is a voiced lingua-alveolar liquid. The tongue tip lifts and touches the alveolar ridge as voiced air is released around the tongue. Children have typically mastered this sound by age 4.

Eliciting L

- Use a mouth model and/or printed visuals and diagrams to teach basic speech anatomy. Focus on the tip of the tongue and alveolar ridge for the /l/ sound.
- Make a tongue out of play-dough and demonstrate how the tip of the tongue lifts up.
- Give step-by-step placement instructions.
    1. **Lift the tongue tip to the alveolar ridge.The sides of your tongue will not lift.**
    2. **Keeping your tongue tip in place, turn your voice on for the /l/ sound.**
- Rub the alveolar ridge with a lollipop or dental swab and instruct the child to lift their tongue tip to the place you rubbed. If you use a lollipop, they will be able to taste the flavoring on their alveolar ridge.
- "Magic Marshmallow" trick. Place a small amount of marshmallow fluff on the child's alveolar ridge and instruct them to elevate their tongue tip, sticking it into the fluff. Tell them to keep it there, as if it is stuck. Then, tell them to turn their voice on and see if the /l/ sound "magically appears".

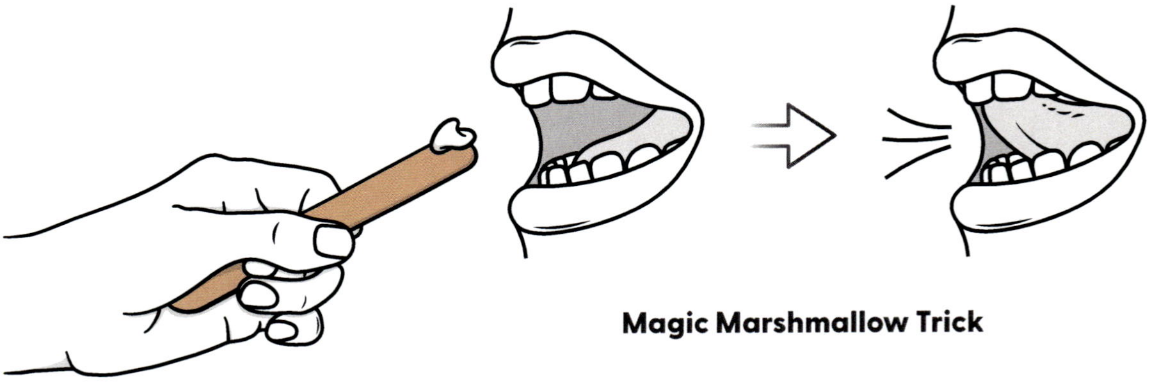

Magic Marshmallow Trick

- Rename the /l/ sound. You can call it the sing-song-sound ("La La La") as you practice. Start by having the child sustain the /a/ sound and then tell them to lift the tongue tip to the alveolar ridge and then drop it down. This may sound like "Ah-La". Then repeat the tongue movement quickly to achieve "La La La".
- Shape from the /d/ sound. Ask the child to make the /d/ sound. Then, tell them to put their tongue tip up and get ready to say /d/, but don't actually release the tongue from the alveolar ridge. Tell them to keep the tongue in place and turn their voice on for a sustained /l/ sound.
- Say "Doll". Start by instructing the child to say /da/ and then while sustaining the vowel, slowly lift their tongue tip up to the alveolar ridge. This should result in them saying what sounds like the word doll.
- If the child is substituting /w/ for /l/, you can instruct them to smile slightly as they are practicing to inhibit lip rounding.
- You can tape mouth visuals for /w/ and /l/ to the therapy mirror to contrast the lip positions, as a reminder to produce the "Tongue-Up Sound" instead of the "Round-Lip-Sound".
- Say this little chant about the L sound. Lyrics: Tongue goes up! Up, up for L! Scan the QR code for the video of this chant.

Scan this QR code to go directly to our free video

PEACHIE SPEECHIE'S

Speech Sound Handbook

The R Sound (Bunched)

/ɹ/
bunched

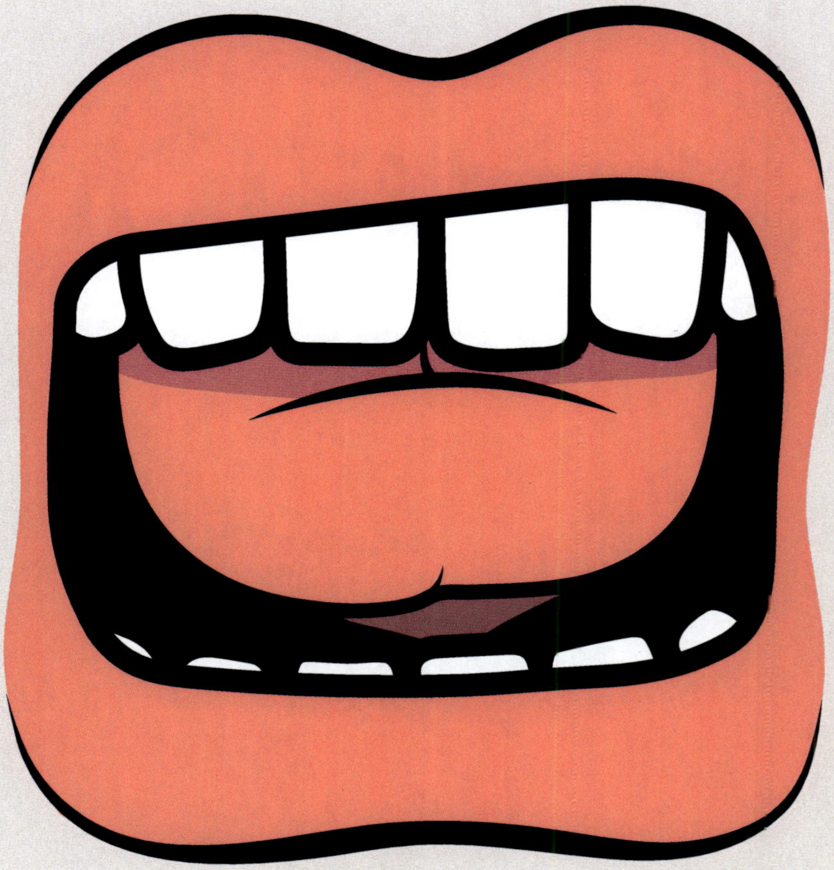

How to Say the R Sound (Bunched)

- Lift the back sides of your tongue to the insides of your back teeth.
- Slide your tongue back, keep it high, and make it tense.
- Turn your voice on.

The R Sound (Retroflex)

/ɹ/
retroflexed

How to Say the R Sound (Retroflex)

- Lift the tip of your tongue and curl it back in your mouth.
- The back sides of your tongue will be lifted too.
- Turn your voice on.

PEACHIE SPEECHIE'S

Speech Sound Handbook

The R Sound

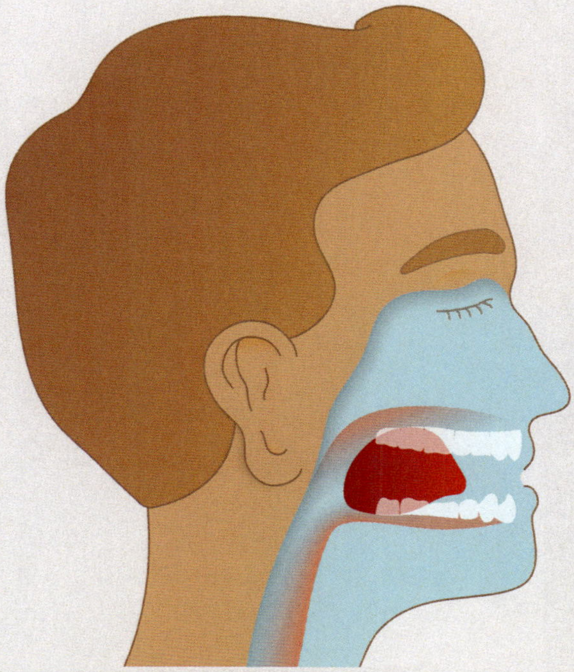

Bunched R

- The back sides of the tongue are lifted to touch the insides of the back teeth.
- The body of the tongue is lowered.
- The tongue root is retracted.
- The front part of the tongue is slightly elevated.

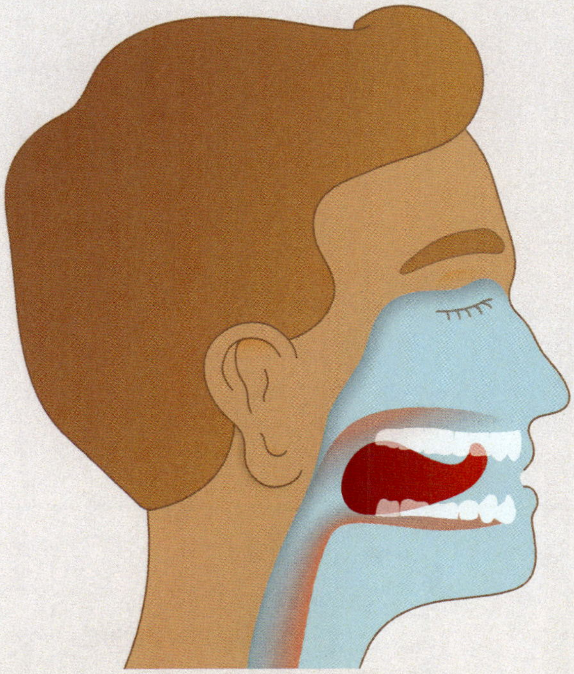

Retroflex R

- The back sides of the tongue are lifted to touch the insides of the back teeth.
- The body of the tongue is lowered.
- The tongue root is retracted.
- The tongue tip elevates and curls back.

Scan this QR code to see our Bunched vs. Retroflex video

SCAN ME

PEACHIE SPEECHIE'S

Speech Sound Handbook

/ɹ/ Word List

Initial Prevocalic

1 Syllable

Race	Rent	Row
Rack	Rice	Rub
Rag	Rich	Rude
Rain	Ride	Ruff
Rake	Right	Run
Ramp	Ring	Rush
Ranch	Rinse	Wrap
Rang	Ripe	Wreath
Rap	Risk	Wreck
Rash	Road	Wrist
Rat	Robe	Wrong
Raw	Rock	Wrote
Reach	Roll	
Read	Roof	
Red	Root	
Reef	Rope	
Reels	Rot	

2 Syllables

Rabbit	Refuse	Wrapping
Raccoon	Relax	Wrestle
Rachel	Relief	Wrinkle
Racket	Remote	Written
Radish	Rescue	
Raffle	Resort	
Rainbow	Revise	
Raisin	Ribbon	
Random	Riddle	
Rapid	Roasting	
Reading	Robot	
Ready	Rocket	
Reason	Rolling	
Recall	Rootbeer	
Recite	Rotten	
Reduce	Rowboat	
Refill	Running	

3 Syllables

Radio	Reunion
Rattlesnake	Romantic
Realize	Runaway
Rebellious	
Recognize	
Recommend	
Rectangle	
Recycle	
Reduction	
Reelect	
Relative	
Religion	
Remedy	
Removal	
Republic	
Resident	
Respectful	

Blends

Bread	Dry	Train
Bring	From	Tree
Brought	Friday	Triangle
Brown	Friend	Truck
Crack	Frog	Trash
Crayon	Frown	
Crown	Grade	
Crumb	Grandpa	
Cry	Grapes	
Dragon	Groceries	
Draw	Ground	
Drink	Practice	
Drive	Pretzel	
Drop	Prince	
Drum	Prize	

Medial Intervocalic

The second syllable in the word begins with /r/

Around	Hearing
Barrel	Hero
Berry	Lyric
Boring	Married
Cairo	Narrow
Carry	Parent
Cherry	Parrot
Correct	Pirate
Dairy	Porridge
Every	Siren
Fairy	Spirit
Forest	Vary
Garage	Worried
Giraffe	

Vocalic AR

Are	Park
Aren't	Shark
Arm	Start
Army	Tarp
Art	Bar
Ark	Car
Alarm	Far
Barn	Jar
Bark	Star
Charge	Tar
Dark	
Garlic	
Hard	
Heart	
Large	

Vocalic ER

Earth	First	Turn	Hour	Stir
Early	Heard	After	Number	Sure
Earn	Learn	Either	Over	Teacher
Bird	Nurse	Fur	Paper	Water
Fern	Person	Her	Purr	Weather

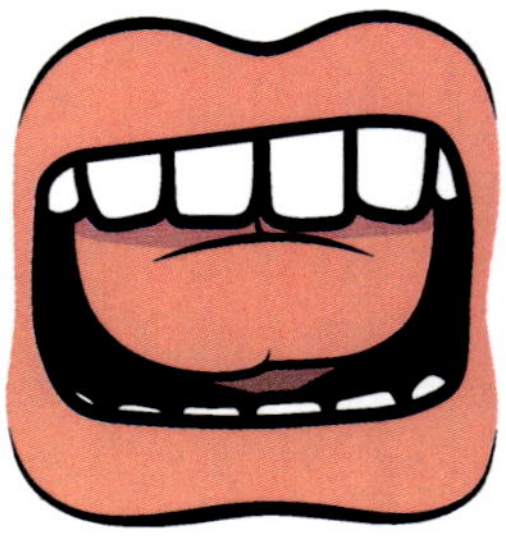

PEACHIE SPEECHIE'S

Speech Sound Handbook

/ɹ/ Word List

Vocalic AIR

Air
Aaron
Airplane
Arrow
Asparagus
Married
Berry
Dairy
Parent
Aware
Bear
Care
Compare
Dare
Fair
Hair
Lair
Mare
Pear
Tear
There
Square
Stare
Where

Vocalic EAR

Ear
Eerie
Earring
Earphones
Irritated
Cafeteria
Cereal
Cheering
Beard
Hero
Period
Pierced
Pyramid
Weird
Cashier
Cheer
Chandelier
Disappear
Fear
Gear
Hear
Near
Pier
Steer
Year

Vocalic IRE

Irene
Irish
Ireland
Iron
Iris
Firewood
Pliers
Tired
Siren
Admire
Buyer
Campfire
Choir
Dire
Empire
Fire
Flyer
Liar
Sapphire
Sire
Tire
Umpire
Vampire
Wire

Vocalic OR

Orange
Organic
Ornament
Oregon
Origin
Boring
Coral
Corn
Forest
Florence
Foreign
Glory
Horse
Moral
Morning
Porridge
Shorts
Sports
Door
Four
Floor
Pour
Shore
Store
Tore

Final RL

Carle
Curl
Earl
Girl
Gnarl
Hurl
Pearl
Swirl
Twirl
Whirl
World

Challenge

Multiple positions within the word

Aardvark
Airport
Barber
Birthmark
Briar
Dryer
Orchard
Earthworm
Firefighter
Perform
Rather
Record
Report
Resort
Tractor
Treasure
Supermarket
Weimaraner
Whirlybird

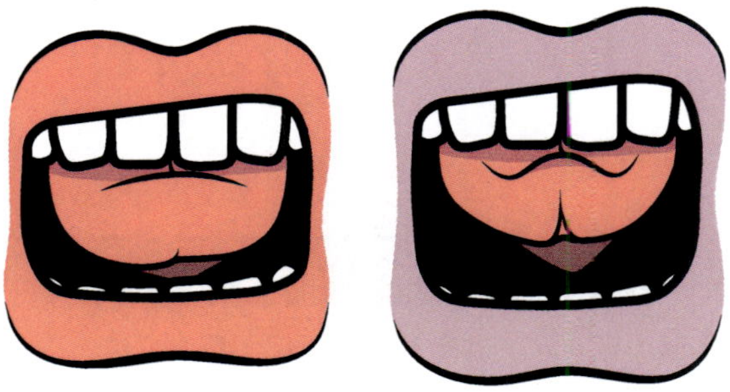

Eliciting /ɹ/ (Bunched)

R is a voiced palatal liquid sound. There are two main tongue shapes that can result in an accurate /ɹ/ sound: Bunched and Retroflex. To produce bunched /ɹ/, the back lateral margins of the tongue lift up to touch the insides of the back teeth. The center of the tongue is lowered, creating a midline groove. The blade of the tongue lifts a little bit. The voiced airstream is directed over the tongue. To produce retroflex /ɹ/, the tongue tip lifts almost to the alveolar ridge and curls back a little bit. The back lateral margins of the tongue lift also. The voiced airstream is directed over the tongue. Children have typically mastered this sound by age 5.

Note that lip rounding is sometimes present during production of the R sound, but it is not a key articulatory requirement.

Eliciting Bunched R

- Use a mouth model and/or printed visuals and diagrams to teach basic speech anatomy.
- Focus on the "tongue bracing spots" inside the back teeth, the back lateral margins of the tongue, tongue tip, and tongue blade for the R sound.
- Give step-by-step placement instructions.
    1. **Lift the back sides of the tongue up to touch the insides of the back teeth. The sides will be up, but the middle will be down, creating a groove.**
    2. **Lift the front of your tongue just a little bit.**
    3. **Make your tongue tight and pull it back a little bit as you turn your voice on for the R sound.**
- Make a play-dough tongue and form it into the shape of a bunched tongue. Lift the back sides up. Show how a midline groove runs down the center.

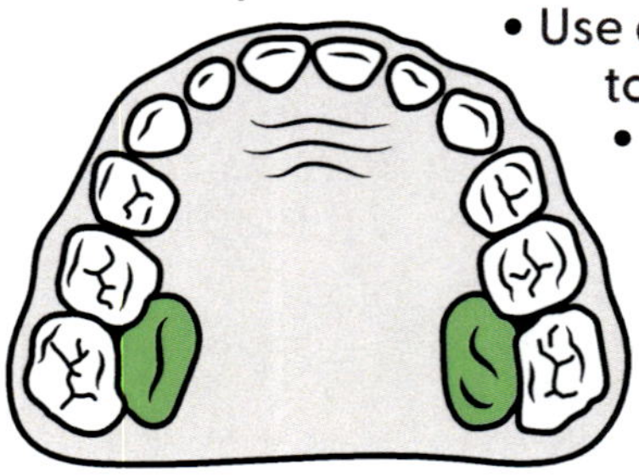

- Use a lollipop or dental swab to rub the back lateral margins of the tongue and insides of back teeth to encourage lateral bracing.
- Using a mouth model, place play dough on the "tongue bracing spots" inside the back teeth, as shown, to show the child where they need to anchor their tongue.
- Tell the child to make a "wide tongue" that spreads out, touching the insides of the back teeth.
- Taco Tongue! Tell the child you need them to make the "taco tongue position". Their tongue will be shaped like a taco shell, with the sides up and the middle lowered. Scan the QR code below for the video about Taco Tongue.

- Shape from the /i/ sound. Start by asking the child to sustain the /i/ sound. Then, instruct them to pull their tongue back, keeping the sides up. The /i/ sound should change, and it will sound like they are saying "ear". Scan the QR code below for a video about shaping from /i/.
- Shape from /ʃ/. Start by asking the child to sustain the /ʃ/ sound. Then, instruct them to pull their tongue back and turn their voice on. The sound should change, and it will sound like they are saying "sure". Scan the QR code below for a video about shaping from /ʃ/.

Taco Tongue — SCAN ME
Shaping from /i/ — SCAN ME
Shaping from /ʃ/ — SCAN ME
Bunched R — SCAN ME

Scan these QR codes to go to our free videos

Eliciting /ɹ/ (Bunched)

Continued

- Shape from /ʒ/. Similar to shaping from /ʃ/, as mentioned on the previous page, have the child start by sustaining /ʒ/ and then pull their tongue back to achieve an R sound. You can target words with the /ʒɚ/ sound combination such as measure, treasure, and closure.
- Use dental flossers to teach tongue placement. Gently place a dental flosser, floss-side-up, into the mouth to push the tongue back. Give additional verbal prompts as needed (back sides of tongue up, blade elevated a bit, voice on, etc.) as you practice with the flosser.
- Using a bite block can help the child differentiate tongue and jaw movement and prevent jaw sliding. If you do not have an actual bite block, you can use a tongue depressor or straw. Place the bite block in the child's mouth between the molars on one side. Have them gently bite to hold it in place. Practice tongue movement for the R sound, using a mirror and light to help them see inside their own mouth.
- Stick Trick for R.
    1. **Ask the child to smile and open their mouth a little.**
    2. **Place the tongue depressor horizontally in their mouth, as pictured below.**
    3. **Ask them to place the tip of their tongue on the edge of the stick in their mouth.**
    4. **Prompt them to lift the back sides of their tongue up to touch the insides of their back teeth and turn their voice on for R.**

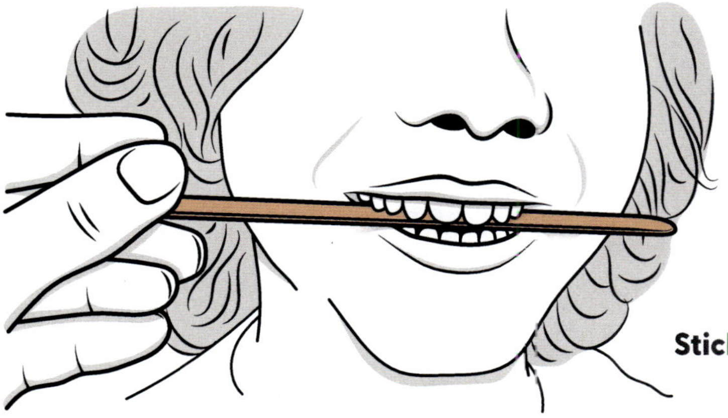

Stick Trick for R

- Door Trick for R. Have the child stand in a doorway. Tell them they are going to pretend to be a tongue in a mouth. Tell them to lift their arms, pressing their palms out into the door frame, just as the back sides of a tongue lift and press into the insides of their back teeth during production of the R sound. Have them do this as they practice saying the R sound.
- Ball Trick for R. Ask the child to reach their arms out long in front of them, interlacing their fingers. Have them pull their arms up and back, mimicking the movement of the tongue for R. Then, give them a large playground ball and have them repeat the motion, squeezing the ball and saying the R sound at the same time. They will feel tension as they squeeze. Scan the QR code below for a video about the Ball Trick for R.
- Don't say R! Rename the R sound and tell the child you are working on the "hiding turtle sound" instead. Instruct them to pull their tongue back into their mouth just like a turtle pulls its head into its shell. Then, tell them to put

Ball Trick

SCAN ME

Scan this QR code to go directly to our free video

Eliciting /ɹ/ (Bunched)

Continued

the back sides of their tongue resting inside their back teeth, just like a sleepy turtle might do if they want to rest their head inside their shell. Once they have their tongue in turtle-position, tell them to turn their voice on. Scan the QR code below for a video about Renaming the R Sound.
Other names to call the R sound: Pirate Sound (Arrrgh!), Rooster Sound (Err Err Err!), Growling Bear Sound (Grrrr), or Revving Engine Sound (RRrrr).

- Use hand motions to represent tongue movement. You can even wear a pink glove to draw attention to it and make it seem more tongue-like. Move the hand up and back as you bend your fingers to show a bunched tongue shape. If you have a large plastic mouth model, you can place your hand inside it as you show movement.
- Visualization. Tell the child to imagine that there are ropes tied to the back of their tongue, pulling the back sides up and back. You could also tell the child to imagine there is a train track along the roof of their mouth and they need to slide the lateral margins of their tongue back along the track.
- Coarticulation for Eliciting Vocalic R. Coarticulation is the idea that the sounds you produce are impacted by other sounds around them. If a child is able to say initial prevocalic R, but having difficulty with final vocalic R, this can be an effective strategy to elicit vocalic R. To do this, select sets of words that end in vocalic R and start with prevocalic R. For example, CAR→RED. Start by saying CA→RED, and gradually blend the words together to say CAR-RED, with a clear vocalic R sound. Scan the QR code below for a video about Coarticulation.
- Practice blends to facilitate placement. If the child needs to work on elevating the back of the tongue, /kɹ/ and /gɹ/ blends can help facilitate that. If they need to lift the blade more, /dɹ/ blends are a good choice. If they need to focus on lateral bracing, try /ʃɹ/ blends.
- Say, "Eureka!" The word eureka can facilitate an accurate R because the sounds preceding R require elevation of the lateral margins of the tongue.
- If a child is substituting /w/ for /ɹ/, instruct them to smile a little bit and use their tongue, not their lips, as they practice. Select target words that start with /ɹi/ (ex: Read, Reach) to inhibit lip rounding.
- Say this little chant about the bunched R. Lyrics: Slide it back, Make it bunched, Make it tight! Scan the QR code for the video of this chant.

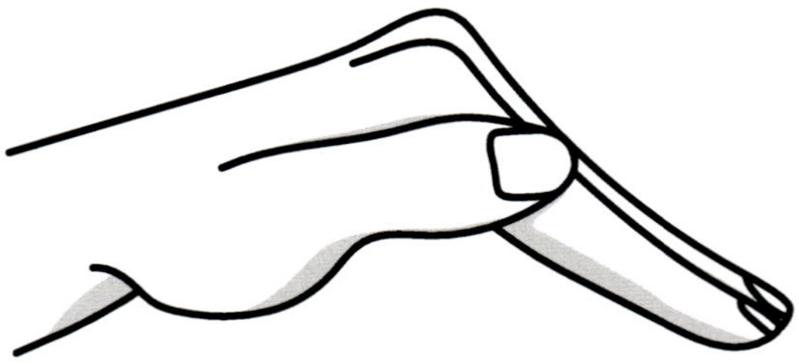

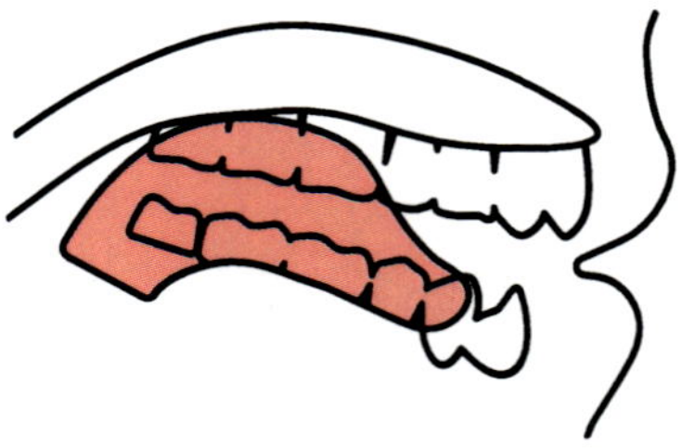

Use hand motions

Renaming
SCAN ME

Coarticulation
SCAN ME

Scan these QR codes to go directly to our free videos

Eliciting /ɹ/ (Retroflex)

R is a voiced palatal liquid sound. There are two main tongue shapes that can result in an accurate /ɹ/ sound: Bunched and Retroflex. To produce bunched /ɹ/, the back lateral margins of the tongue lift up to touch the insides of the back teeth. The center of the tongue is lowered, creating a midline groove. The tip/blade of the tongue lifts a little bit. The voiced airstream is directed over the tongue. To produce retroflex /ɹ/, the tongue tip lifts almost to the alveolar ridge and curls back a little bit. The back lateral margins of the tongue lift also. The voiced airstream is directed over the tongue. Children have typically mastered this sound by age 5.

Note that lip rounding is sometimes present during production of the R sound, but it is not a key articulatory requirement.

The tips below are specific to the retroflex /ɹ/. Many of the tips listed on the Eliciting Bunched R page can also be helpful when working on retroflex /ɹ/, especially for addressing lateral bracing. SLPs are encouraged to read through all of the tips on both pages for the R sound.

Eliciting Retroflex R

- Use a mouth model and/or printed visuals and diagrams to teach basic speech anatomy.
- Focus on the "tongue bracing spots" inside the back teeth, the back lateral margins of the tongue, tongue tip, and tongue blade for the R sound.
- Give step-by-step placement instructions.
  1. **Lift the tip of your tongue up, almost touching your alveolar ridge.**
  2. **Curl your tongue tip back. The back sides of your tongue will be up too.**
  3. **Turn your voice on for the R sound.**
- Make a play-dough tongue and form it into the shape of a retroflex tongue. Lift the tip up and curl it back. Scan the QR code for the video about play-dough tongues for the R Sound.
- Using a bite block can help the child differentiate tongue and jaw movement and prevent jaw sliding. If you do not have an actual bite block, you can use a tongue depressor or straw. Place the bite block in the child's mouth between the molars on one side. Have them gently bite to hold it in place. Practice tongue movement for the retroflex R sound, lifting the tongue tip and curling it back slightly with the bite block in place. Use a mirror and light to help them see inside their own mouth.
- Rename the R sound. You can call the retroflex R the curling sound, the backward sound, or the tongue-tip-sound as you practice.
- Say, "Karla!" This is a popular word to facilitate an accurate retroflex R. Start by saying, "Ka-La", "Ka-La", gradually moving the tongue tip further back on the palate each time so that KaLa becomes Karla.
- Talk Like a Pirate. Instruct the child to sustain /a/ as they look in the mirror. Then, ask them to slowly lift their tongue tip up and curl it back while continuing to sustain /a/. Ask them to close their jaw a little bit and listen as the sound changes. This will sound like they are saying, "Arrrr".

Make a play dough tongue

Play-Dough Tongues

SCAN ME

Retroflex R

SCAN ME

Scan these QR codes to go directly to our free videos

Eliciting /ɹ/ (Retroflex)

Continued

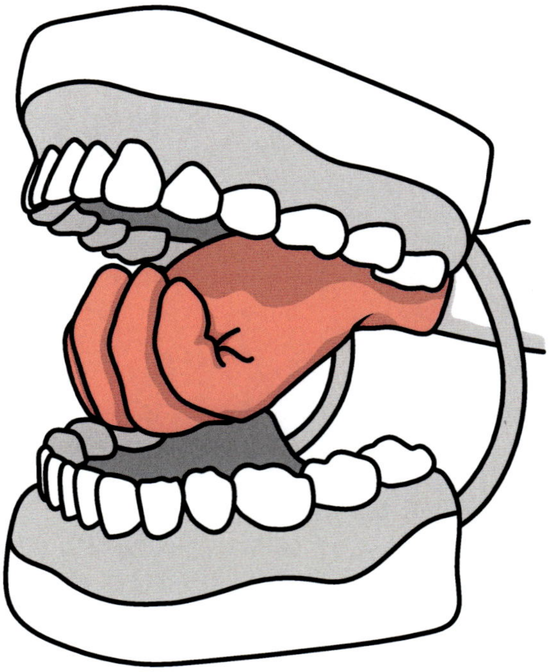

- Use hand motions to represent tongue movement. You can even wear a pink glove to draw attention to it and make it seem more tongue-like. Place your hand palm-up, and curl your fingertips up and back. If you have a large plastic mouth model, you can place your hand inside it as you show movement.
- Hold your arm straight out in front of you with a tight fist. Bend your elbow to curl your arm back, representing how the tongue curls back for a retroflex R.
- Shaping from /l/. Start by instructing the child to place the tongue tip on the alveolar ridge for the /l/ sound. As they sustain /l/, ask them to slide the tip of their tongue back along the roof of their mouth. They will hear the sound begin to change from L to R.
- Tongue Tap Back. This is similar to the above mentioned method of shaping, but instead of sliding the tongue back, you tap the tongue tip back. Start by instructing the child to say /l/ and then move their tongue a little bit behind the alveolar ridge and say /l/ again. Do this repeatedly, tapping further back until L turns to R.
- Use dental flossers to teach tongue placement. Use a flosser shaped like the one pictured here. Gently place a dental flosser in the child's mouth. Ask them to hook their tongue tip around the floss and curl it back. Instruct them to say the R sound with their tongue in this retroflex position.
- Say this little chant about the retroflex R. Lyrics: Tongue Back, Curl the tip, Nice and tight, RRR! Scan the QR code for the video of this chant.

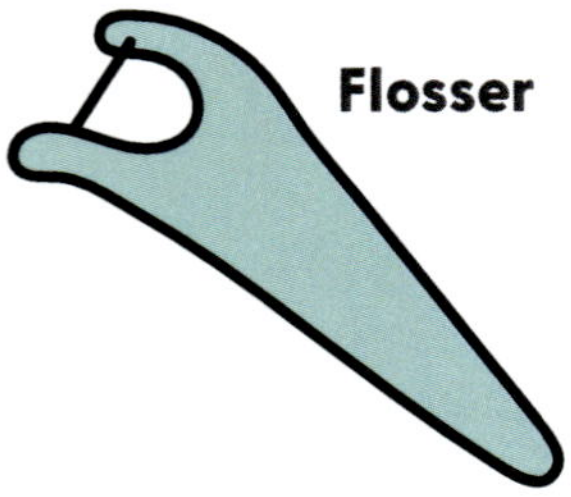

Flosser

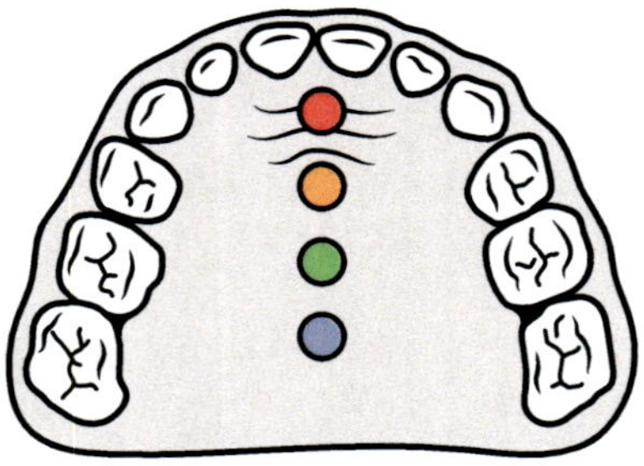

Tapping the tongue tip back from L to R

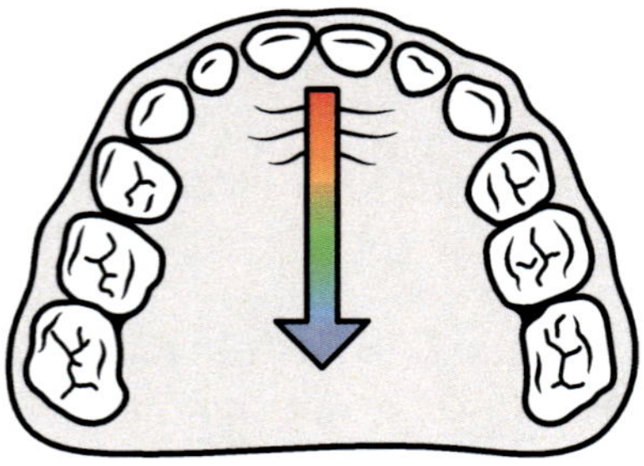

Sliding the tongue tip back from L to R

Retroflex R

SCAN ME

Scan this QR code to go directly to our free video

Teaching Lingual Tension

Production of the R sound requires lingual tension. Here are some ways to teach children about tension.

Tips for Tension

- Have the child lift a heavy book or small weight and observe the muscles in their arm tightening. Explain that the tongue is a muscle, and just like the muscles in the arm, the tongue can get tight, too.
- Model tensing and relaxing your tongue and instruct the child to do it as well, using a mirror to watch their tongue move. Once they can tighten and relax, work on tightening + lateral bracing.
- Use a tongue depressor to stroke the sides of the tongue to encourage the child to tense it.
- Squeeze a squishy toy ("slow-rise squishies" are perfect for this) in your hand. Watch with the child as it gradually expands. Explain that it was tense and now it is relaxing.
- Door Trick for R. This strategy was mentioned on the Bunched R Elicitation page as well. Have the child stand in a doorway. Tell them they are going to pretend to be a tongue in a mouth. Tell them to lift their arms, pressing their palms out into the door frame, just as the back sides of a tongue lift and press into the insides of their back teeth during production of the R sound.
- The Chair Grab. Have the child sit in a sturdy chair and grab he sides of the chair. When they practice their R sound, have them pull upward on the chair. This illustrates the lifting motion of their tongue lifting to touch the inner back molars, and also lets them experience tension in their arms. Tell them you want them to have a tight feeling in their tongue as well.
- Ball Trick for R. This strategy was mentioned on the Bunched R Elicitation page as well. Ask the child to reach their arms out long in front of them, interlacing their fingers. Have them pull their arms up and back, mimicking the movement of the tongue for R. Then, give them a large playground ball and have them repeat the motion, squeezing the ball and saying the R sound at the same time. They will feel tension as they squeeze.

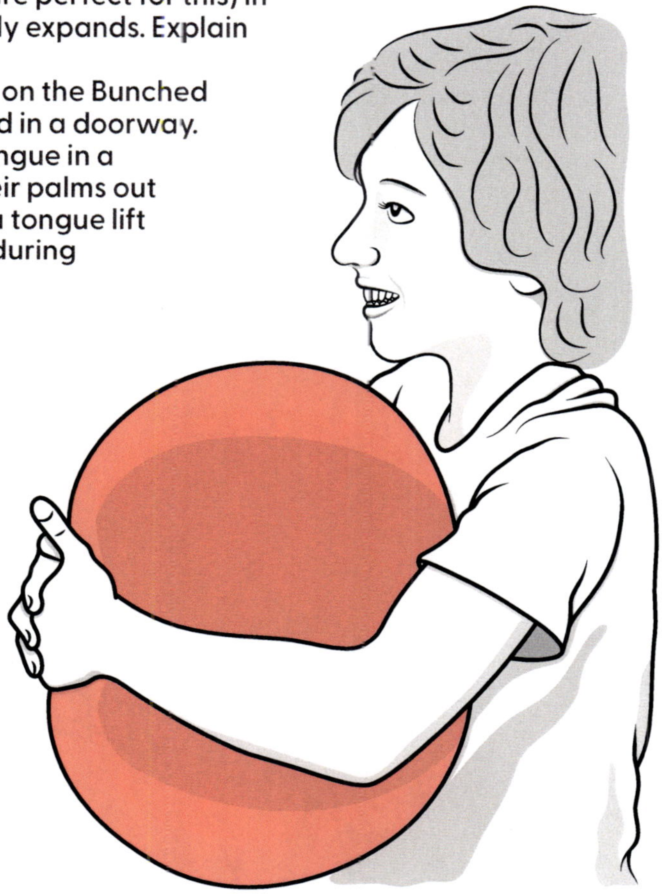

Ball Trick for R

Tension

SCAN ME

Scan this QR code to go directly to our free video

Teaching Lingual Tension

Continued

- Fill a balloon with flour and instruct the child to squeeze it in their hand while pulling their arm up and back. This represents the tongue movement and tension required for R.
- Rubber bands. Hook a rubber band on your right thumb and use three left fingers to pull up and back. Instruct the child to do the same. They will feel the tension of the rubber band which can remind them that they need tension in their tongue.
- Resistance band. This is similar to the rubber band idea, but using a large exercise resistance band. Hold one end of the band and have the child grab the other end with both hands, pulling it back as they practice. This uses a bigger motor movement, which can be helpful for some children.
- Feel the Tension: Instruct the child to place their hand gently on your throat, under your chin. Have them feel while you say "uhh" and then "RRR". They will be able to feel your tongue move as it becomes tense for the R sound. Scan the QR code for the video on teaching children about lingual tension.
- Hula Hoop Trick for R. Have the child stand in the center of a hula hoop as they press their palms out into the sides of the hoop like the tongue presses against the insides of their back teeth during production of R. This is a way to explain tension and lateral bracing for R.

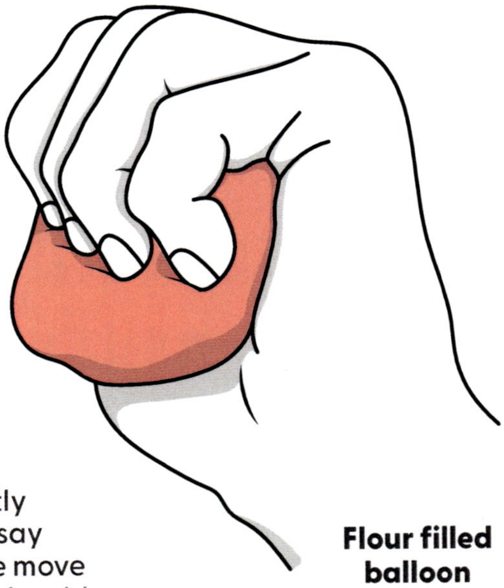

Flour filled balloon

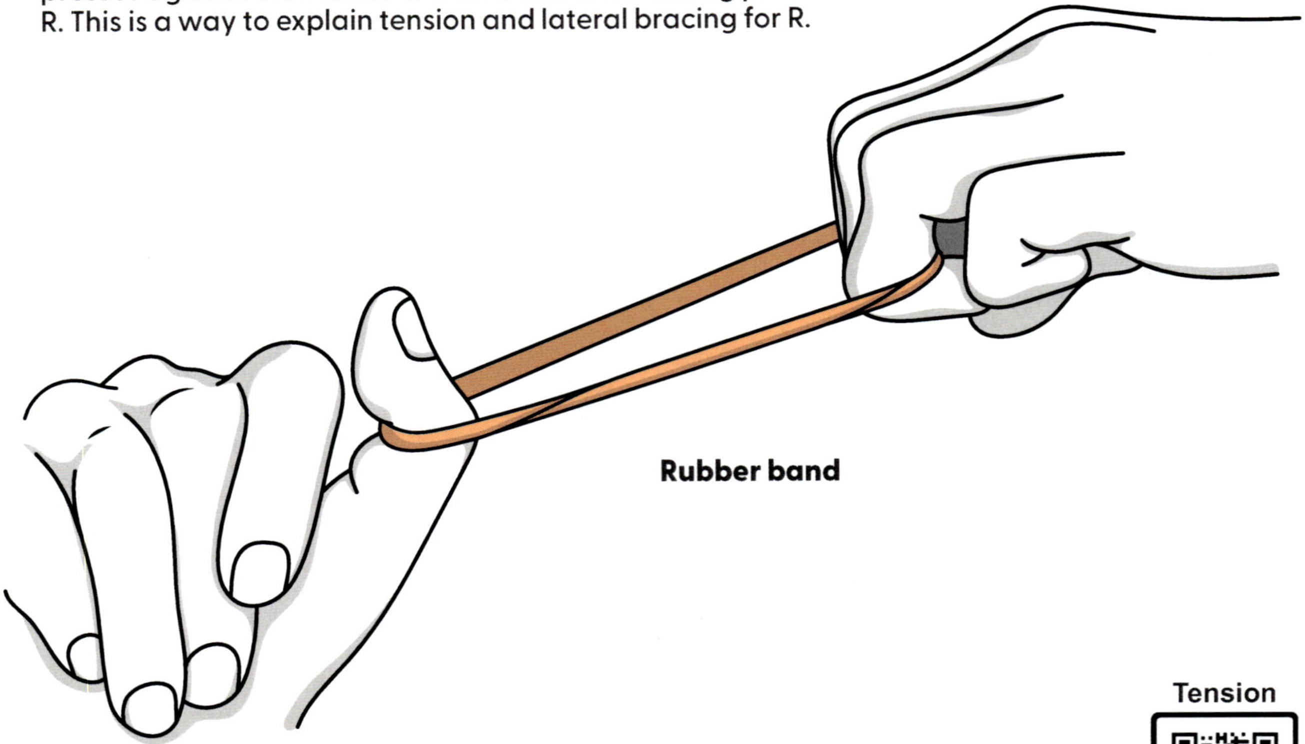

Rubber band

Tension

SCAN ME

Scan this QR code to go directly to our free video

Vowels

Vowels

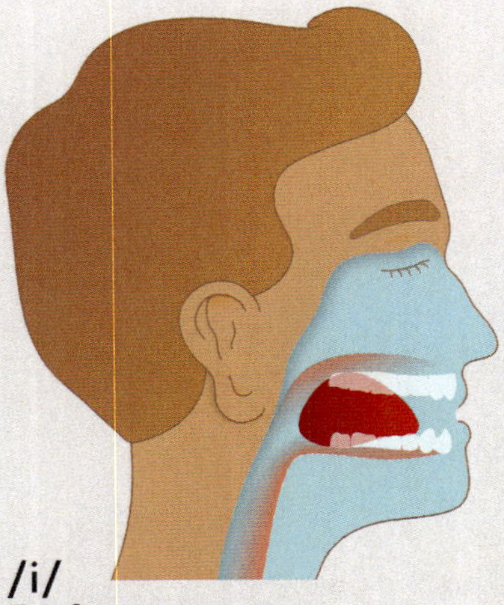

/i/
Ex: feet, mean
- Sides of tongue are lifted, touching upper teeth.
- Front of tongue is lifted, and tip can be behind lower teeth.
- Lips are retracted.

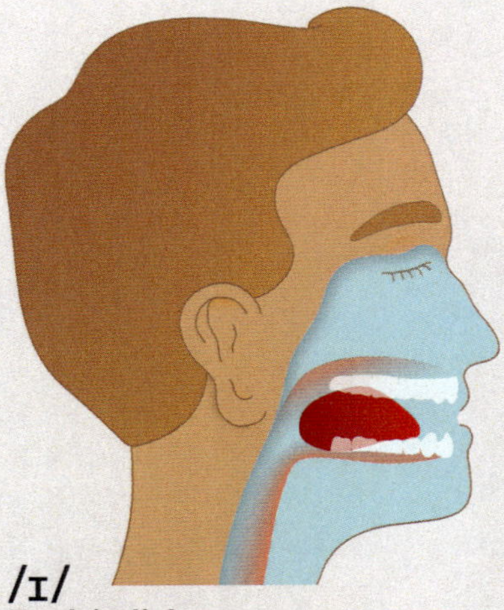

/ɪ/
Ex: hit, lid
- Sides of tongue are lifted, touching upper teeth.
- Front of tongue is lifted, but not as much as for /i/.
- Lips are slightly retracted.

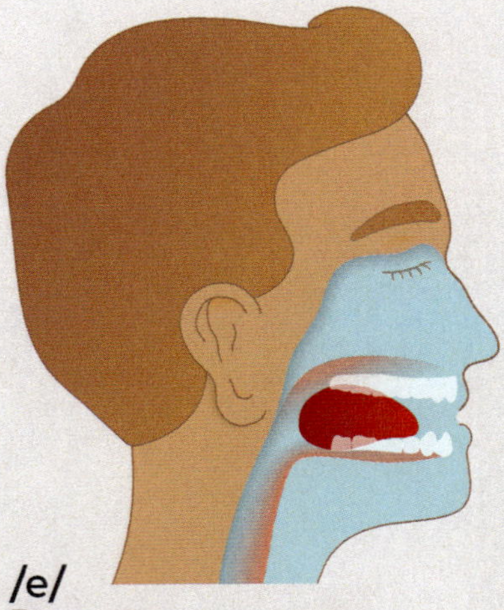

/e/
Ex: cape, name
- Sides of tongue are lifted, touching upper teeth.
- Front of tongue is raised slightly lower than for /ɪ/.
- Lips are unrounded and might be very slightly retracted.

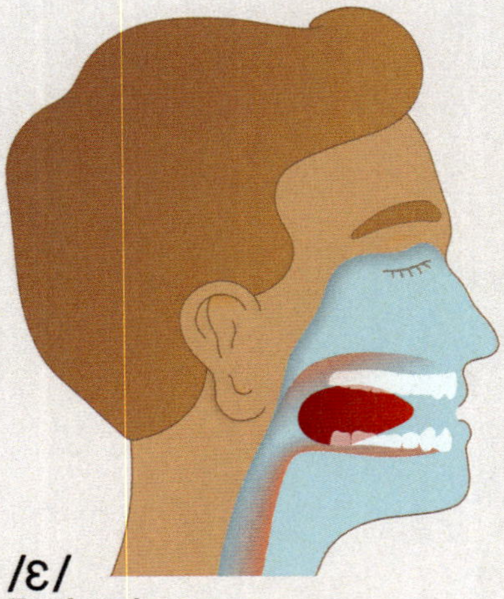

/ɛ/
Ex: bed, pet
- Sides of tongue are lifted, touching upper teeth.
- The front of the tongue is slightly raised.
- Lips are in a neutral position and the jaw is slightly lowered.

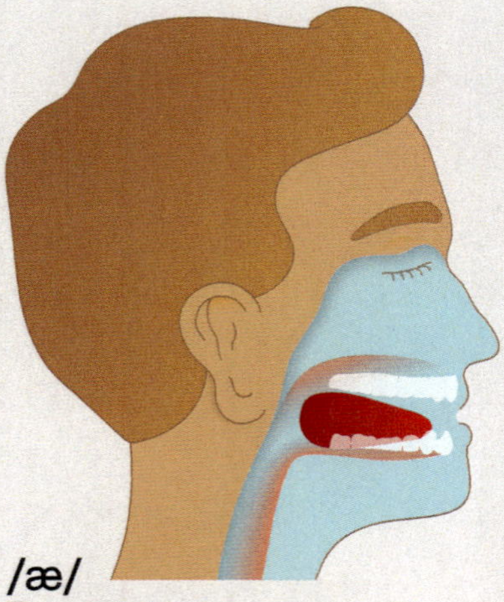

/æ/
Ex: cat, tap
- The tongue does not touch the upper teeth.
- The tip of the tongue is slightly raised.
- The lips are slightly drawn back and the jaw is slightly lower than for /ɛ/.

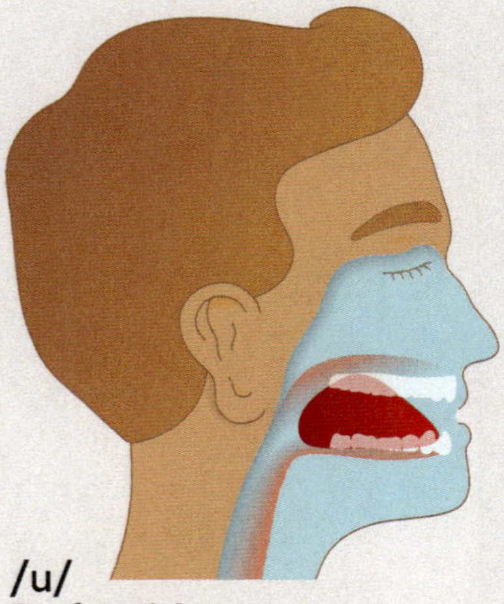

/u/
Ex: food, boot
- The back of the tongue is raised high toward the palate, but doesn't touch the palate.
- The lips are very rounded and the jaw is in a neutral position.

Vowels

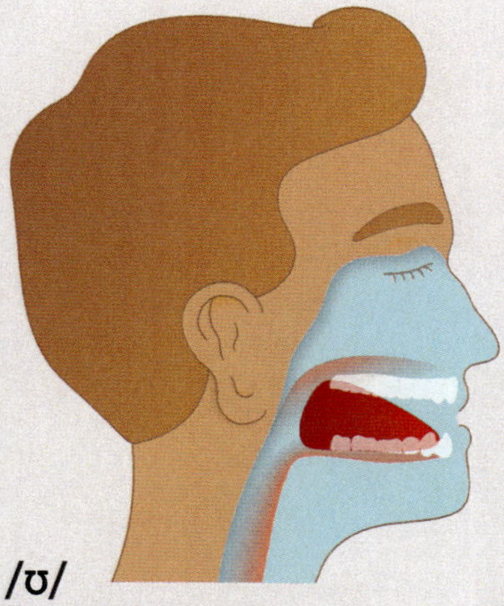

/ʊ/
Ex: could, book
- The back of the tongue is raised toward the palate, slightly lower than for /u/.
- The lips are rounded and the jaw is in a neutral position.

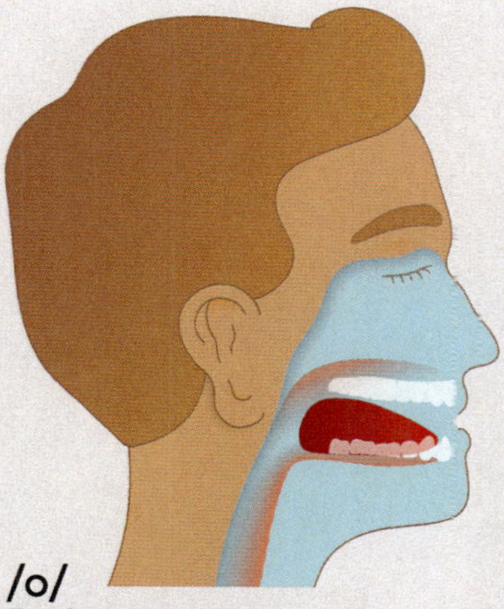

/o/
Ex: bone, nose
- The back of the tongue is lifted slightly.
- The lips are rounded and open.
- The jaw is slightly lowered.

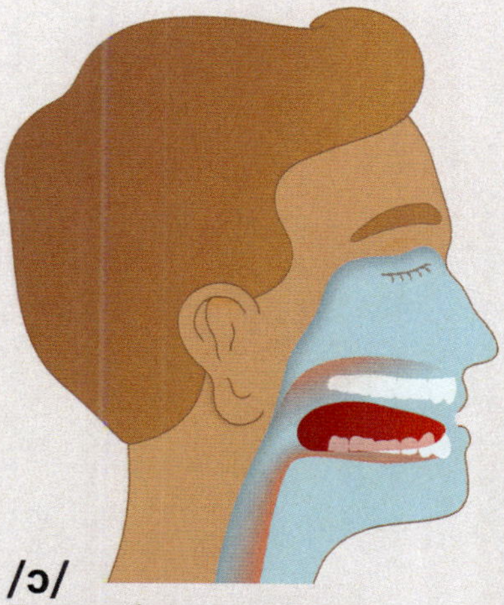

/ɔ/
Ex: awful, taught
- The back and middle of the tongue is raised.
- The tongue tip rests low.
- The lips are rounded and protrude forward a bit.
- The jaw is lowered.

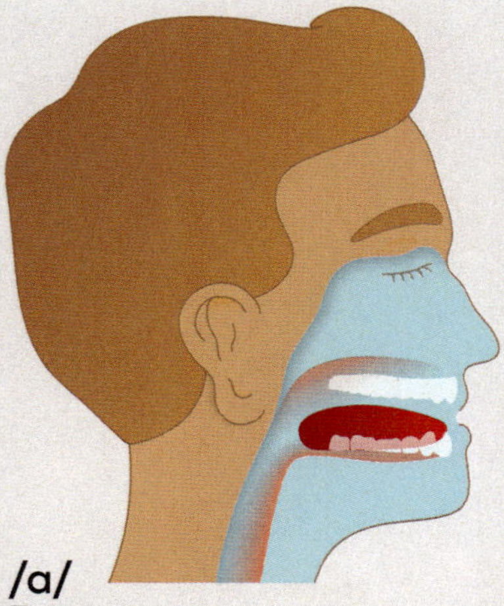

/ɑ/
Ex: top, pot
- The tongue rests low in the mouth.
- The lips are relaxed and unrounded.
- The jaw is lowered.

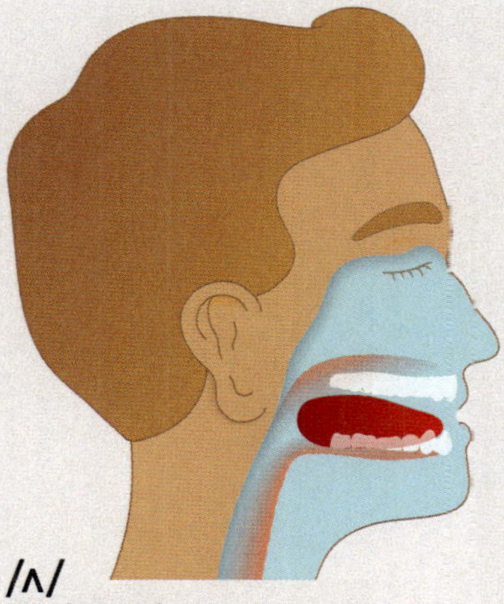

/ʌ/
Ex: bun, love
- The center of the tongue is slightly raised.
- The front of the tongue rests on the floor of the mouth.
- The lips are unrounded and neutral.
- The jaw is also in a neutral position.

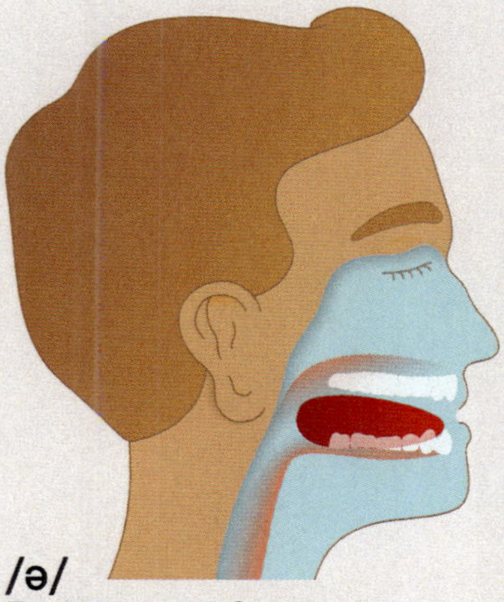

/ə/
Ex: amount, focus
- The middle of the tongue is flat, not touching the teeth.
- The lips are unrounded and neutral.
- The jaw is also in a neutral position.

PEACHIE SPEECHIE'S

Speech Sound Handbook

The /i/ Sound

/i/

How to Say the /i/ Sound

- Lift the back sides of your tongue.
- The blade of the tongue is lifted a little bit.
- Tongue is tense.
- Turn your voice on.

PEACHIE SPEECHIE'S

Speech Sound Handbook

/i/ Word List

Initial

Eager
Eagle
Ears
Eat
Eaten
Easel
East
Easter
Ego
Egypt
Emu
Equal
Eve
Even
Evening
Evil
Ian

Medial

Asleep
Beach
Bead
Bean
Beaver
Beet
Beetle
Breathing
Cheese
Cheetah
Chief
Complete
Feast
Feed
Feet
Fleece
Freeze
Extreme
Green
Heat
Here
Hero
Jeans
Jeep
Keep
Leaf
Least
Leep
Marine
Mean
Meat
Medium
Need
Niece
Peel
Peep
Piece
Queen
Reach
Recess
Reef
Seem
Seek
Sheet
Sincere
Sleet
Speech
Street
Sweet
Teach
Team
Teen
These
Theme
Treat
Vegan
Veto
Weak
Yield

Final

Agree
Baby
Bee
Candy
Chilly
Coffee
Copy
Daisy
Dusty
Empty
Every
Free
Happy
He
Hockey
Journey
Knee
Key
Me
Monkey
Pea
Pretty
Puppy
See
She
Sunny
Tea
The
Three
Tree
Twenty
We
Windy
Worry

Eliciting /i/

/i/ is a high, front, tense, unrounded vowel. The tongue is lifted, with the back lateral margins touching the top teeth. The lips are retracted and the voice is turned on to produce /i/.

Keep in mind that different regional dialects impact how vowels are pronounced. There may be some variation among your clients for this reason.

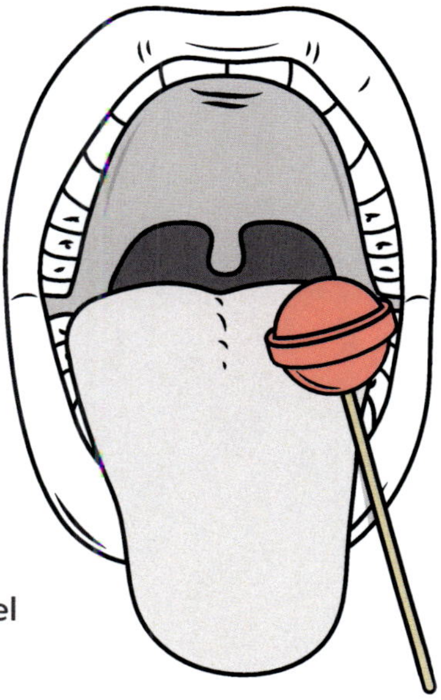

Eliciting /i/

- Use a mouth model and/or printed visuals to describe tongue placement in the mouth for /i/.
- Give step-by-step placement instructions.
  1. **Put the sides of your tongue up, touching the upper teeth.**
  2. **Lift the blade of your tongue up a little, but not touching the hard palate.**
  3. **Turn your voice on to let the sound out.**
- Rub the back lateral margins of the tongue and insides of upper back teeth with a lollipop or tongue depressor to increase awareness of articulators. Instruct the child to lift the sides of their tongue up for /i/.
- Look in a mirror with the child and alternate between /u/ and /i/, drawing attention to lip rounding vs. lip retraction for /i/.
- Spread your lips and point to the corners of your mouth as you model /i/ to emphasize the lip retraction. Ask the child to repeat after you, pointing to the corners of their own mouth in the mirror.
- Hold your hand out flat by your mouth and then lift it up, as a reminder to lift the tongue up for /i/.
- Place your thumb and index finger just above the upper lip toward the outer edges of the lips as you instruct the child to say /i/. This is a reminder for them to lift the sides of the tongue up and retract the lips.
- If the child is having difficulty with tongue tension, practice tensing and relaxing the tongue in the mirror and then instruct them to place the lateral margins of the tongue up and make them tense for /i/.
- Rename the /i/ sound. You can call it the scared sound (Eeee!), the happy smile sound, or the tiny mouse sound as you practice.
- Once /i/ has been established, you can ask the child to sustain /i/ and then gradually open their jaw wider and wider. Their tongue will gradually drop lower as they do this. This results in production of other vowels as their jaw lowers, and may assist in teaching other vowel sounds.

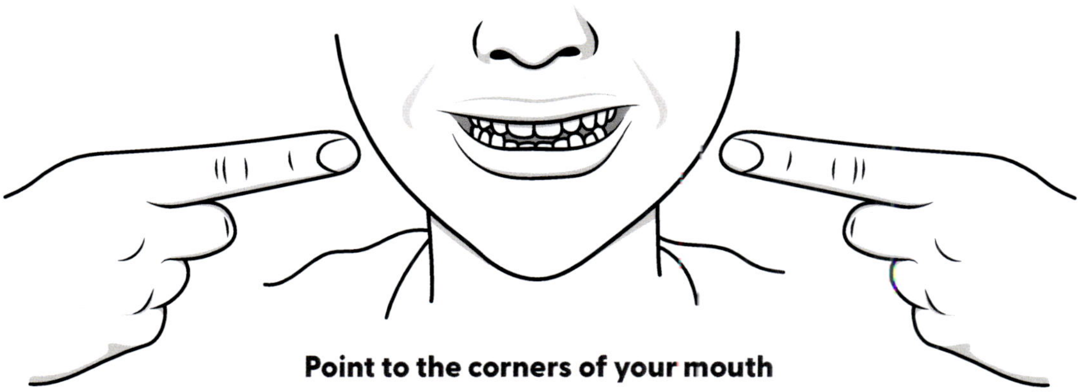

Point to the corners of your mouth

The /ɪ/ Sound

/ɪ/

How to Say the /ɪ/ Sound

- Lift the back sides of your tongue up.
- Raise the front of your tongue a little bit.
- Turn your voice on.

/ɪ/ Word List

Initial

Icky
If
Ill
Image
Impossible
Important
Impress
In
Inch
Ink
Insect
Instant
Interest
Into
Invent
Invite
It
Itch

Medial

Bid
Big
Bin
Bit
Chin
Chip
Did
Dip
Fig
Fill
Fin
Fit
Flip
Get
Gift
Grid
Him
Hip
Hit
Kid
Kitty
Lid
Lip
Miss
Mint
Mitt
Mix
Pick
Pig
Pin
Pinch
Pit
Quit
Quick
Rich
Rip
Shin
Sit
Six
Skin
Spit
Twin
Will
Win
Winter
Wig
Yip

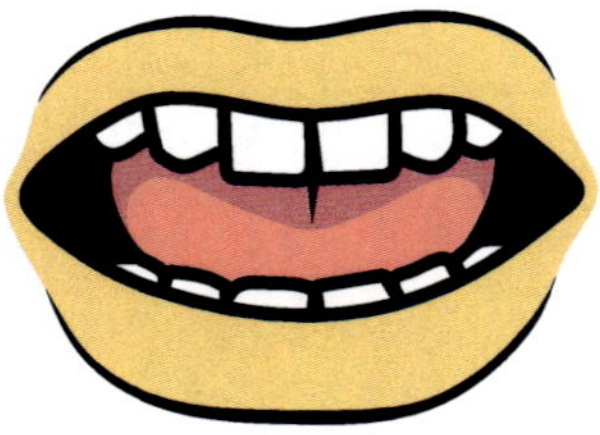

PEACHIE SPEECHIE'S

Speech Sound Handbook

Eliciting /ɪ/

/ɪ/ is a high, front, tense, unrounded vowel. The tongue lifts up toward the palate, with lateral margins touching the upper teeth. The tongue is not quite as high as it is for the /i/ sound. The lips are retracted and the voice is turned on to produce /ɪ/.

Keep in mind that different regional dialects impact how vowels are pronounced. There may be some variation among your clients for this reason.

Eliciting /ɪ/

- Use a mouth model and/or printed visuals to describe tongue placement in the mouth for /ɪ/.
- Look in a mirror with the child and model the /ɪ/ sound, using a flashlight to help them view the tongue. Ask them to lift their mouth like yours and attempt /ɪ/.
- Hold your hand out flat by your mouth and then lift it up, as a reminder to lift the tongue up for /ɪ/.
- Start by having the child sustain /i/ and then have them lower their jaw slightly for /ɪ/.
- Rename the /ɪ/ sound. You can call it the yucky sound (as in "ick!") as you practice.

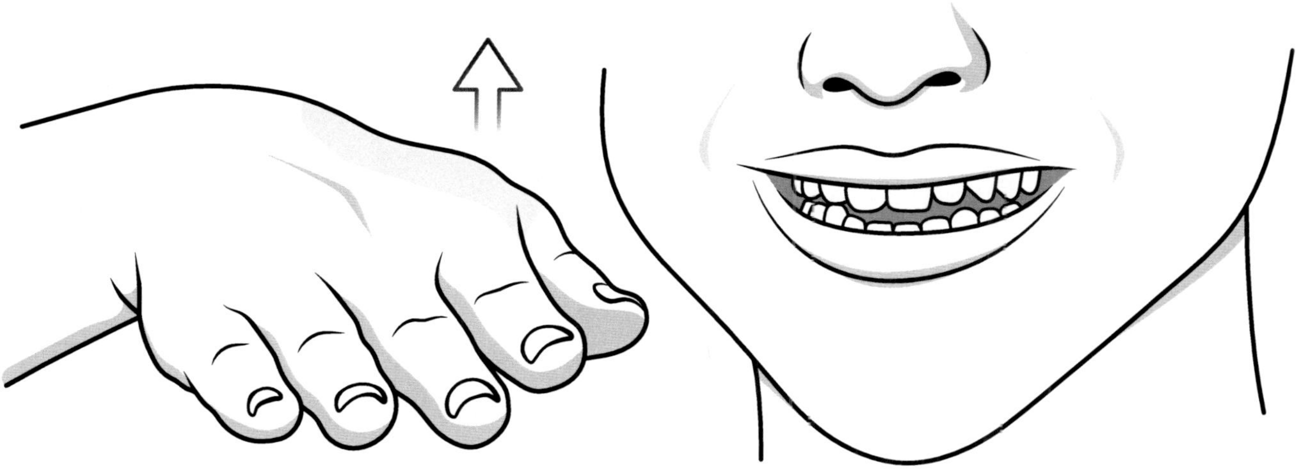

Lift your hand

PEACHIE SPEECHIE'S

Speech Sound Handbook

The /e/ Sound

/e/

How to Say the /e/ Sound

- Open the mouth slightly.
- Raise the front of the tongue.
- The sides of the tongue will touch the upper teeth.
- Turn your voice on.

PEACHIE SPEECHIE'S

Speech Sound Handbook

/e/ Word List

Initial

Abe
Ace
Ache
Acorn
Aid
Age
Ale
Aim
Ape
Apron
Air
Ate

Medial

Baby
Bacon
Bake
Basic
Cage
Cake
Came
Crazy
Face
Fade
Fake
Fame
Flake
Game
Halo
Make
Maple
Name
Naval
Lady
Lake
Pail
Paint
Paper
Plane
Play
Radio
Rain
Same
Shade
Shaky
Space
Stage
Table
Tail
Take
Trade
Train
Wake
Wave

Final

Bay
Clay
Day
Gray
Hay
Jay
Kay
Lay
May
Neigh
Obey
Pay
Play
Pray
Ray
Relay
Say
Spray
Stay
Survey
They
Today
Tray
Way
Yay

Eliciting /e/

/e/ is a mid, front, tense, unrounded vowel. The mouth is open slightly with unrounded lips. The sides of the tongue are lifted to touch the upper teeth. The front of the tongue is raised toward the palate a little bit.

Keep in mind that different regional dialects impact how vowels are pronounced. There may be some variation among your clients for this reason.

Eliciting /e/

- Use a mouth model and/or printed visuals to describe tongue placement in the mouth for /e/.
- Start by having them sustain /i/ and then have them lower their tongue and jaw a little bit. Listen as the sound changes, and shape into the /e/ sound.
- Look in a mirror with the child and model the /e/ sound, using a flashlight to help them view the tongue. Ask them to make their tongue like yours and attempt /e/.
- Use a hand motion to represent the sound. You can start by holding your thumb and index fingers a few inches out from the corners of your mouth. You can produce the /eɪ/ diphthong, lifting your thumb as you lift your tongue.

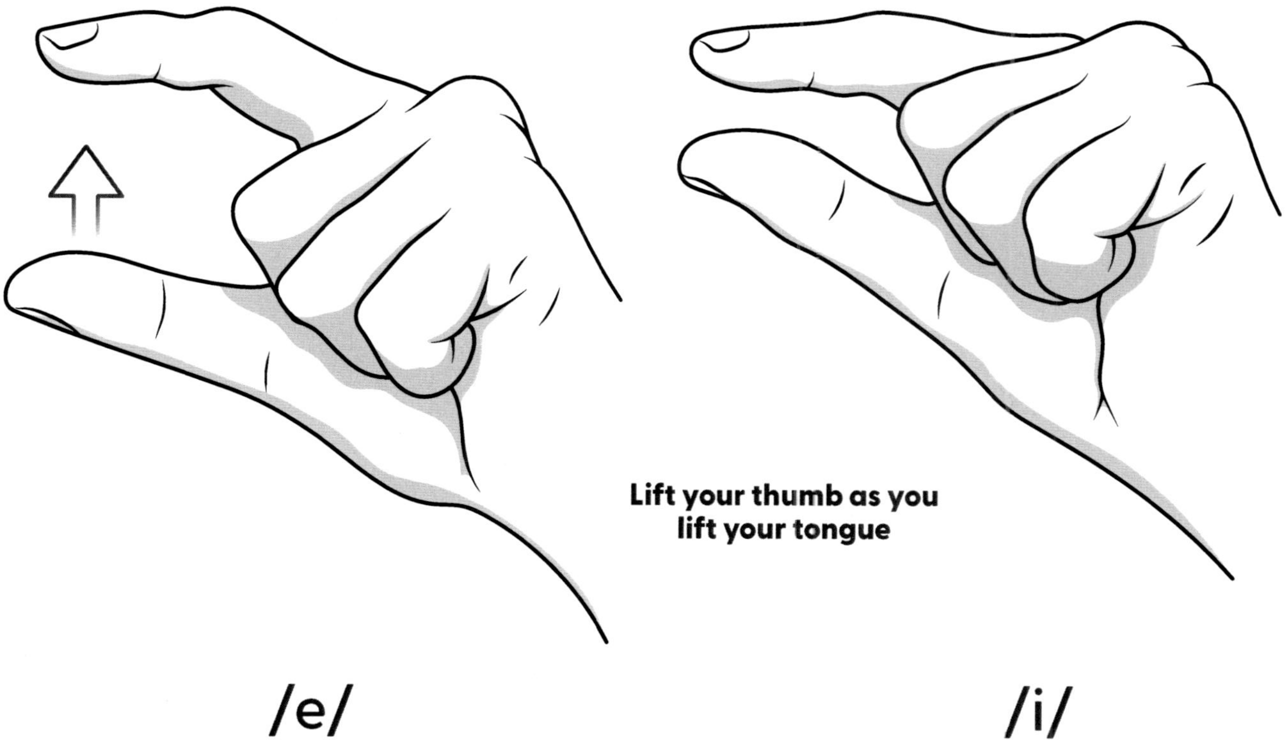

PEACHIE SPEECHIE'S

Speech Sound Handbook

The /ɛ/ Sound

/ɛ/

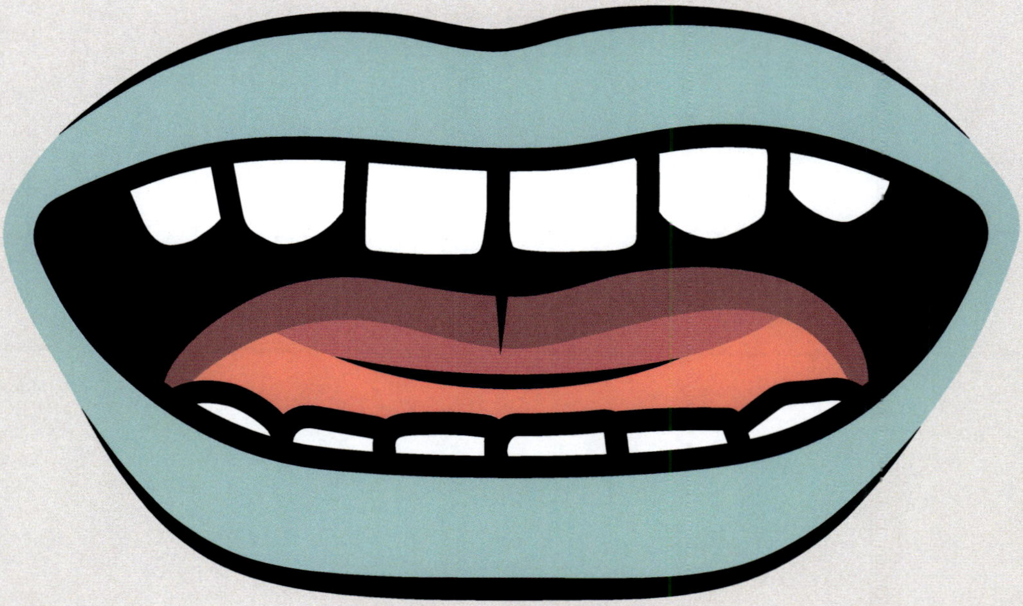

How to Say the /ɛ/ Sound

- Lift the front of the tongue up.
- Keep your lips in a neutral position.
- Slightly lower your jaw.
- Turn your voice on.

/ɛ/ Word List

Initial

Edge
Egg
Elephant
Elf
Elk
Ellie
Emma
End
Engine
Enter
Etch
Evan
Ever

Medial

Bed
Beg
Bell
Bet
Deck
Fell
Friend
Get
Guess
Hen
Jet
Ken
Let
Lept
Men
Mess
Neck
Net
Peck
Pen
Pet
Red
Said
Set
Tell
Ten
Tent
Vest
Well
Wet
Wreck
Yell
Yep
Yes

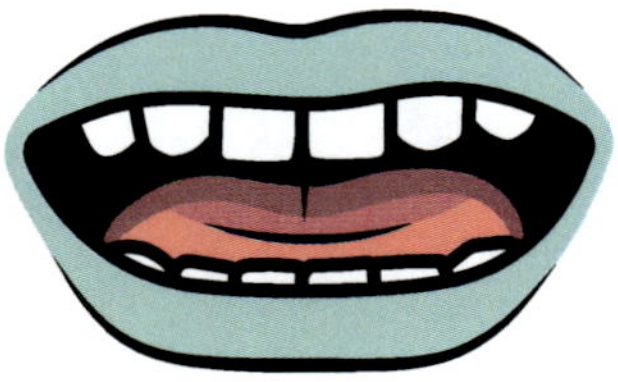

Eliciting /ɛ/

/ɛ/ is a mid, front, lax, unrounded vowel. The front of the tongue is lifted. The lips remain in a neutral position with the jaw slightly lowered. The voice is on to produce the /ɛ/ sound.

Keep in mind that different regional dialects impact how vowels are pronounced. There may be some variation among your clients for this reason.

Eliciting /ɛ/

- Use a mouth model and/or printed visuals to describe tongue placement in the mouth for /ɛ/.
- Look in a mirror with the child and model the /ɛ/ sound, using a flashlight to help them view the tongue. Ask them to make their tongue like yours and attempt /ɛ/.
- Use a hand shape to represent the sound. You can make the sign for "E" in American Sign Language (ASL), held to the side of the mouth as you model the sound.

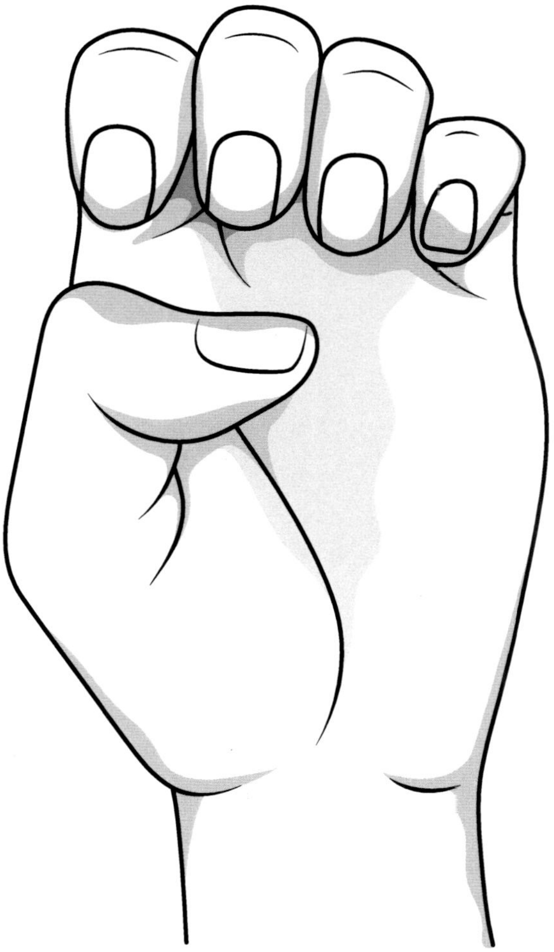

Letter "E" in ASL

The /æ/ Sound

/æ/

How to Say the /æ/ Sound

- Open your mouth.
- Slightly retract your lips.
- Lift the front of the tongue a little.
- Turn your voice on.

PEACHIE SPEECHIE'S

Speech Sound Handbook

/æ/ Word List

Initial

Act
Add
After
Africa
Allison
Ally
An
And
Ant
App
Apple
Ask
Ash
At

Medial

Bad
Bat
Batch
Bath
Band
Cat
Camera
Can
Cap
Cash
Dab
Dad
Damp
Dash
Fad
Fan
Fat
Fast
Gap
Hat
Hand
Happy
Has
Have
Jam
Jacket
Land
Mad
Man
Mat
Match
Math
Nap
Nasty
Natural
Pad
Pat
Patch
Pass
Rabbit
Ran
Ranch
Rat
Rap
Sad
Sat
Snap
Stack
Stamp
Tag
Talent
Tan
Tap
Task
Van
Vat
Yam
Zap

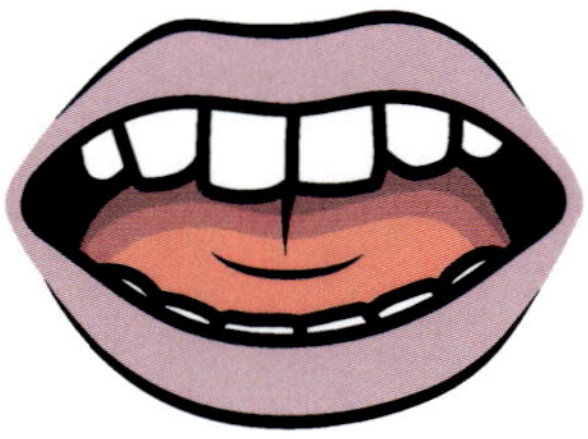

Eliciting /æ/

/æ/ is a low, front, lax, unrounded vowel. The mouth is opened with unrounded lips. The front part of the tongue is raised a little bit.

Keep in mind that different regional dialects impact how vowels are pronounced. There may be some variation among your clients for this reason.

Eliciting /æ/

- Use a mouth model and/or printed visuals to describe tongue placement in the mouth for /æ/.
- Look in a mirror with the child and model the /æ/ sound, using a flashlight to help them view the tongue. Ask them to make their mouth like yours and attempt /æ/.
- Rename the /æ/ sound. You could call it the surprised sound ("Aaa!"), for example, as you practice. This pairs well with a "surprised" hand motion, mentioned below.
- Use a hand cue as a reminder of the vowel. For the /æ/ sound, you can put your hands up on either side of your mouth, palms facing out. You can also use the American Sign Language letter "A" as shown below.
- Start by instructing the child to sustain the /ɛ/ sound. Then, use your thumb and index finger to guide their jaw into a lower position for /æ/.

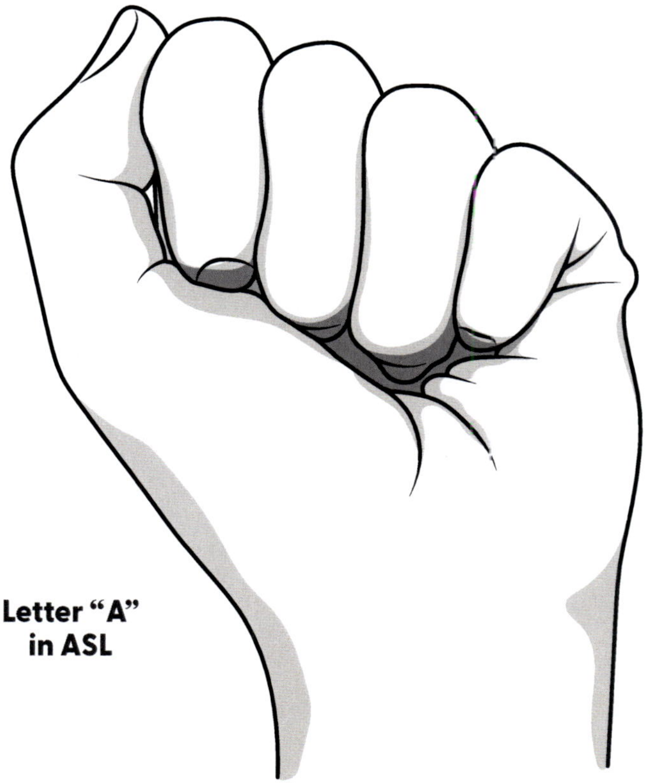

Letter "A" in ASL

The /u/ Sound

/u/

How to Say the /u/ Sound

- Lift the back of the tongue almost to the velum.
- Round your lips (very round!).
- Turn your voice on.

/u/ Word List

Medial

Boom
Boot
Broom
Bruise
Cool
Choose
Chute
Cruise
Duty
Droop
Fruit
Food
Juice
June
Mood
Moon
Ruby
Rude
Rule
Rumor
Shoot
Student
Soon
Suit
Toot
Tooth
Troop
Truth
Tube
Tulip
Tune
Numeral
Whose
Zoom

Final

Avenue
Blue
Brew
Chew
Crew
Dew
Drew
Flew
Goo
Glue
Issue
Jew
Moo
New
Poo
Rue
Screw
Shoo
Statue
Stew
Sue
Through
Tissue
True
Too
Virtue
Who
You
Zoo

Eliciting /u/

/u/ is a high, back, tense, rounded vowel. The back of the tongue lifts high, nearly touching the velum. The lips are rounded. The voice is on to produce the /u/ sound.

Keep in mind that different regional dialects impact how vowels are pronounced. There may be some variation among your clients for this reason.

Eliciting /u/

- Model the /u/ sound and ask the child to look in the mirror and repeat after you.
- Look in a mirror with the child and alternate between /i/ and /u/, drawing attention to lip retracting vs. rounding for /u/.
- Emphasize the lip rounding required for /u/ by pointing to your rounded lips.
- You can use additional hand symbols for /u/ such as pressing your fingers together near your mouth as a reminder to bring the lips together into a rounded position.
- Rename the /u/ sound. You can call it the ghost sound ("Oooo!"), for example, as you practice.
- Shaping from /i/. Start by having them sustain the /i/ vowel while slowly rounding their lips. The sound will change from /i/ to /u/.
- Tell the child to pretend they are going to blow out birthday candles. Then, tell them to turn on their voice for /u/.

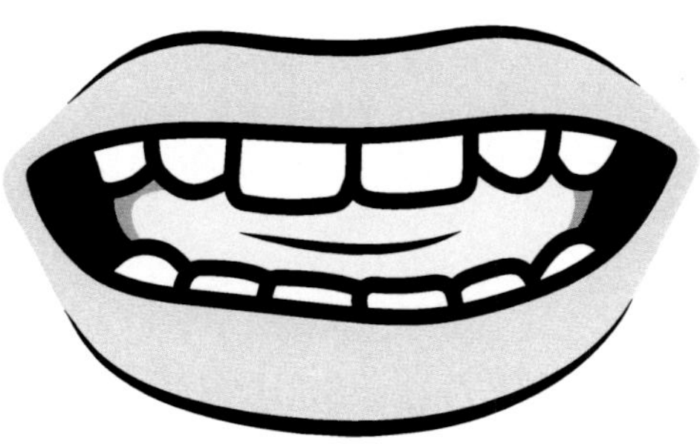

Lips Retracted

Lips Rounded

The /ʊ/ Sound

/ʊ/

How to Say the /ʊ/ Sound

- Raise the back of the tongue.
- Round your lips and push them out a bit.
- Turn your voice on.

PEACHIE SPEECHIE'S

Speech Sound Handbook

/ʊ/ Word List

Medial

Book
Brook
Bush
Butcher
Cook
Cookie
Could
Foot
Full
Good
Goodbye
Nook
Hood
Hoof
Hook
Look
Pudding
Pull
Put
Push
Rook
Should
Shook
Stood
Sugar
Took
Understood
Wood
Woof
Wool
Woman

PEACHIE SPEECHIE'S

Speech Sound Handbook

Eliciting /ʊ/

/ʊ/ is a high, back, tense, rounded vowel. The back of the tongue lifts high, nearly touching the velum. The lips are rounded. The voice is on to produce the /ʊ/ sound.

Keep in mind that different regional dialects impact how vowels are pronounced. There may be some variation among your clients for this reason.

Eliciting /ʊ/

- Model the /ʊ/ sound and ask the child to look in the mirror and repeat after you.
- Shape from the /u/ sound. Start by having the child sustain the /u/ sound. Then ask them to relax their lips a little bit for the /ʊ/ sound. You may also prompt them to drop their tongue a little bit.
- Use a hand symbol as you practice. You can bring your fingers together near your mouth, but not pressed as tightly together as you did for /u/.

/u/

boom, food, tooth

/ʊ/

book, good, woof

PEACHIE SPEECHIE'S

Speech Sound Handbook

The /o/ Sound

/o/

How to Say the /o/ Sound

- Lift the back of the tongue a little.
- Round the lips.
- Turn your voice on.

PEACHIE SPEECHIE'S

Speech Sound Handbook

/o/ Word List

Initial

Oak
Oats
Oboe
Omit
Only
Opal
Open
Own
Ozone

Medial

Boat
Bonus
Broke
Coat
Cone
Cloak
Close
Coach
Coast
Doze
Float
Focus
Goal
Goat
Hole
Home
Hope
Joke
Loan
Locate
Note
Nose
Moment
Phone
Pole
Road
Robe
Smoke
Soap
Sold
Stove
Throat
Toad
Toast
Tone
Yogurt
Vote

Final

Arrow
Banjo
Blow
Bow
Crow
Flow
Go
Glow
Grow
Know
Mow
Low
Piano
Pillow
Slow
Snow
Toe
Window
Yellow

Eliciting /o/

/o/ is a mid, back, tense, rounded vowel. The back of the tongue is elevated a little bit, not all the way to the palate. The lips are rounded and the voice is on.

Keep in mind that different regional dialects impact how vowels are pronounced. There may be some variation among your clients for this reason.

Eliciting /o/

- Model the /o/ sound and ask the child to look in the mirror and repeat after you.
- Use a hand symbol as you practice. You can form a circle with your hand, representing the shape of the lips and also the letter "O".
- Shape from the /u/ sound. Start by asking the child to sustain /u/ and then have them lower their jaw to achieve /o/.

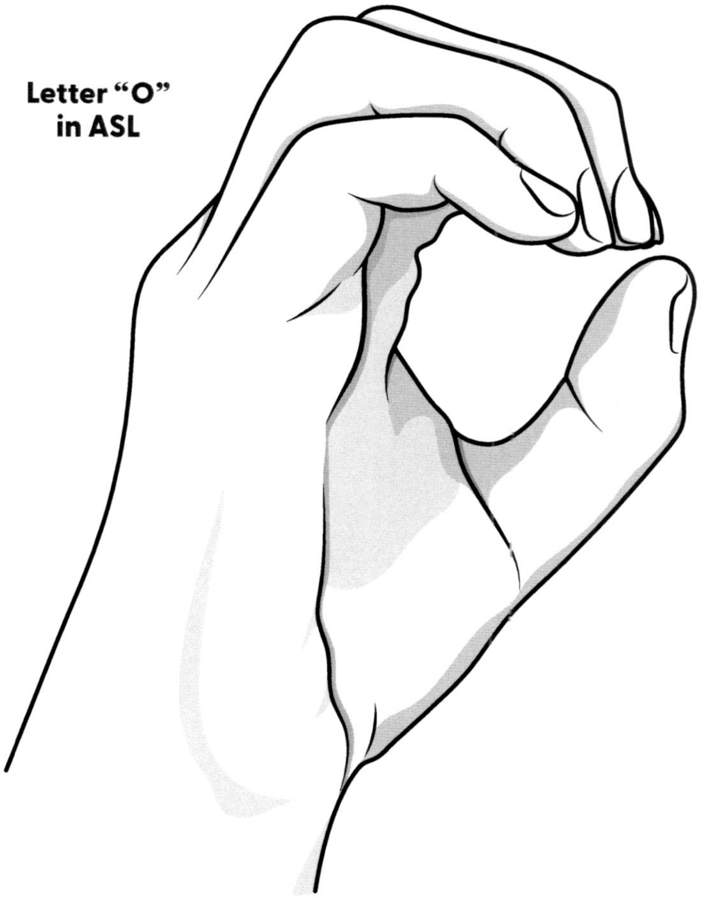

The /ɔ/ Sound

/ɔ/

Many American speakers do not distinguish between /ɔ/ and /a/. For that reason, they will be discussed together in this book.

How to Say the /ɔ/ Sound

- Open your mouth.
- Lower your tongue and jaw.
- Round your lips.
- Turn your voice on.

PEACHIE SPEECHIE'S

Speech Sound Handbook

The /a/ Sound

/a/

Many American speakers do not distinguish between /ɔ/ and /a/. For that reason, they will be discussed together in this book.

How to Say the /a/ Sound

- **Open your mouth.**
- **Lower your tongue and jaw.**
- **Turn your voice on.**

PEACHIE SPEECHIE'S

Speech Sound Handbook

/ɔ/ and /ɑ/ Word List

Many American speakers do not distinguish between /ɔ/ and /ɑ/. For that reason, they will be discussed together in this book.

Initial

Aqua
All
Awe
Awful
Awning
Awesome
Honor
Object
Octopus
Odd
Off
Office
Often
Olive
Oliver
On
Onward
Ostrich
Otter
Ox

Medial

Ball
Bot
Boss
Bottle
Bought
Box
Call
Car
Caught
Cause
Chop
Coffee
Cop
Cost
Cot
Cough
Cross
Dock
Dog
Doll
Dolphin
Dot
Drops
Far
Flop
Fog
Fox
Frog
God
Gone
Got
Hall
Hog
Hop
Hot
Job
Jog
Knock
Lawn
Lock
Log
Long
Lots
Mall
Mom
Mop
Moth
Not
Octagon
Pod
Pop
Pot
Robin
Rocket
Rod
Rot
Salt
Sauce
Shop
Soccer
Sock
Sop
Squash
Star
Swamp
Swan
Talk
Tar
Top
Toss
Tot
Wand
Waffle
Wash
Wasp
Watch
Wrong

Final

Bra
Caw
Claw
Draw
Flaw
Gnaw
Jaw
Law
Paw
Raw
Saw
Slaw
Straw
Thaw

PEACHIE SPEECHIE'S

Speech Sound Handbook

Eliciting /ɔ/ and /ɑ/

/ɔ/ is a mid-low, back, tense, rounded vowel. The jaw is lowered and the tongue remains low in the mouth. The lips are rounded a little bit, and the voice is on.

/ɑ/ is a low, back, tense, unrounded vowel. The jaw is lowered and the tongue remains low in the mouth. The lips are unrounded and the voice is on.

Keep in mind that different regional dialects impact how vowels are pronounced. There may be some variation among your clients for this reason. Many American speakers do not distinguish between /ɔ/ and /ɑ/. For that reason, they will be discussed together in this book.

Eliciting /ɔ/ and /ɑ/

- Model the /ɔ/ or /ɑ/ sound and ask the child to look in the mirror and repeat after you.
- Give instructions to lower the jaw and the tongue. Once their mouth is open, instruct them to turn on their voice to make the sound.
- Place your thumb and index finger on the chin just below the lower lip. Gently bring the jaw downward to encourage the open-mouthed position required for /ɔ/ and /ɑ/.
- Tell them to open their mouth and say, "ahh", just like they do at the doctor's office. Tell them they need to open wide enough so you can see inside their mouth.
- Rename the sound. You can call it the "relaxing sound" or the "open-mouth" sound while you practice.

/kɔfi/

/kɑfi/

PEACHIE SPEECHIE'S

Speech Sound Handbook

The /ʌ/ Sound

/ʌ/

How to Say the /ʌ/ Sound

- Open your mouth.
- Relax your lips.
- Let the tip of your tongue rest low in your mouth.
- Breathe out with your voice on.

The /ə/ Sound

/ə/

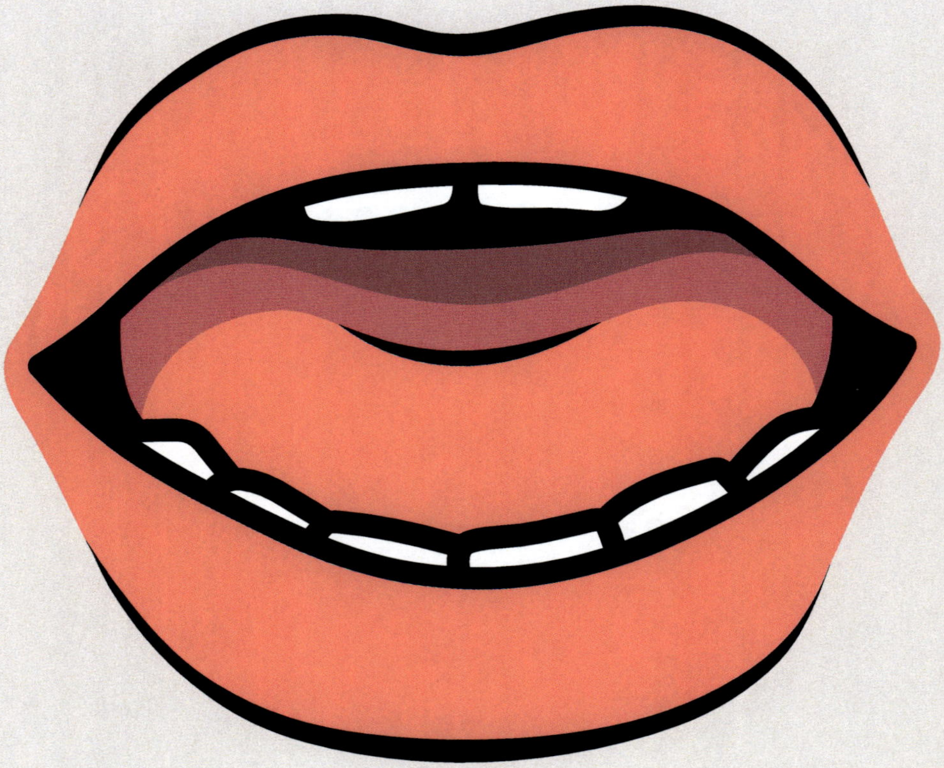

How to Say the /ə/ Sound

- Open your mouth.
- Relax your lips.
- Let the tip of your tongue rest low in your mouth.
- Breathe out with your voice on.

/ʌ/ and /ə/ Word List

Initial /ʌ/

Udder
Under
Uncle
Up
Us
Utmost

Medial /ʌ/

Above
Blood
Bug
Bun
Bunch
Bus
But
Buzz
Cluck
Cub
Cup
Cut
Does
Done
Duck
Dud
Dust
Enough
Flood
Fudge
Fun
Fuss
Glove
Gum
Gun
Gus
Hum
Hut
Love
Lump
Month
Must
Mutt
Nut
Puff
Rub
Ruff
Rug
Run
Scrub
Such
Sum
Sun
Touch
Tough
Tug
Was
What
Won
Wug
Young

Initial /ə/

About
Account
Across
Again
Ago
Alike
Alive
Alone
Amaze
Amount
Announce
Around
Away
Awake
Occur
Offend
Upon

Medial /ə/

Accident
Album
Algebra
Atlas
Balloon
Banana
Blanket
Camel
Campus
Carrot
Celebrate
Children
Comma
Confess
Easily
Elephant
Enemy
Festival
Focus
Formal
Freedom
Human
Idea
Item
Lemon
Magazine
Parrot
Pencil
Ribbon
Suggest
Supply
Thousand
Voluntary
Zebra

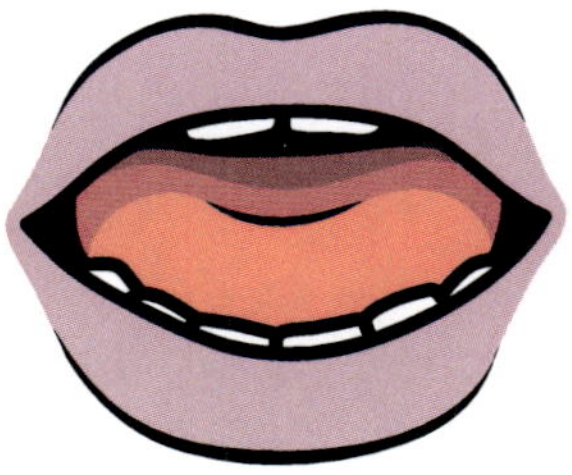
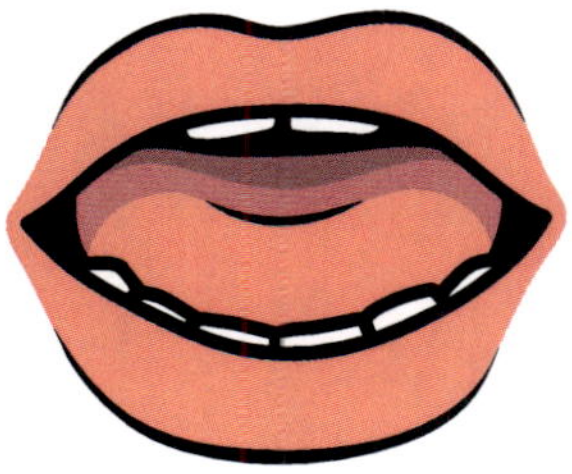

PEACHIE SPEECHIE'S

Speech Sound Handbook

Eliciting /ʌ/ and /ə/

/ʌ/ is a low, central, lax, unrounded vowel. The mouth is open, with the front of the tongue resting low. The lips are relaxed and the voice is on.

/ə/ is a mid, central, lax, unrounded vowel. The mouth is open, with the front of the tongue resting in a central position. The lips are relaxed and the voice is on. /ə/ is a shorter, unstressed vowel and is often referred to as the schwa.

Keep in mind that different regional dialects impact how vowels are pronounced. There may be some variation among your clients for this reason.

Eliciting /ʌ/ and /ə/

- Model the /ʌ/ sound and ask the child to look in the mirror and repeat after you. As the child is voicing, give prompts to pull the tongue back a little while keeping the tongue tip low.
- Use your thumb and index finger to gently lower the child's jaw as they turn their voice on.
- Rename the /ʌ/ sound. You can call it the thinking sound, as if someone is saying, "uhhh" and trying to think of what to say. Or, you could call it the upset sound as if someone is saying, "uh!" in disappointment.
- Frequently model the /ʌ/ sound during therapy activities. For example, making an airplane go <u>up</u>, <u>up</u>, <u>up</u>. Encourage the child to model after you.

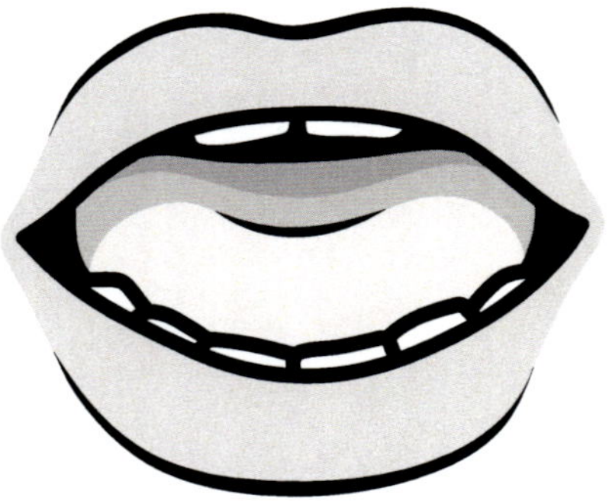

/ʌ/
Stressed

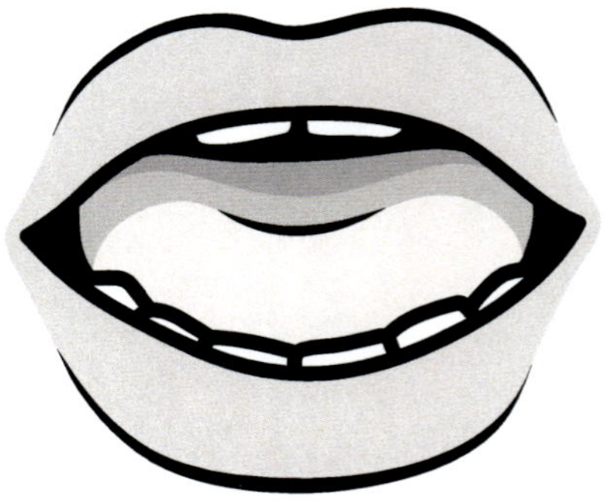

/ə/
Unstressed

"I want to be a schwa... it's never stressed."

/ə/ Never Stressed

Dipthongs

PEACHIE SPEECHIE'S

Speech Sound Handbook

The /aɪ/ Sound

/aɪ/

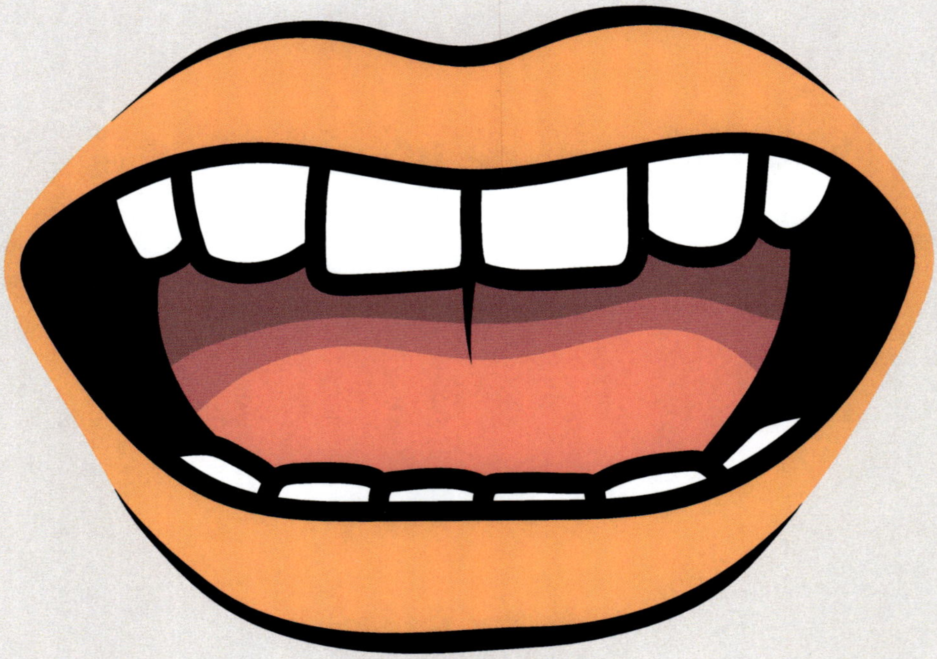

How to Say the/aɪ/ Sound

Starting position:
- Lower your jaw.
- Lips open wide.
- Tongue tip low.
- Breathe out with your voice on.

→

Ending position:
- Raise your tongue and jaw.
- Spread your lips.

PEACHIE SPEECHIE'S

Speech Sound Handbook

The /aʊ/ Sound

/aʊ/

How to Say the/aʊ/ Sound

Starting position:
- Lower your jaw.
- Lips open wide.
- Tongue tip low.
- Breathe out with your voice on.

→

Ending position:
- Raise your tongue
- Move your lips into a rounded position.

PEACHIE SPEECHIE'S

Speech Sound Handbook

The /ɔɪ/ Sound

/ɔɪ/

How to Say the/ɔɪ/ Sound

Starting position:
- Round your lips.
- Pull your tongue back.
- Breathe out with your voice on.

→

Ending position:
- Pull your tongue up and forward.
- Spread your lips.

PEACHIE SPEECHIE'S

Speech Sound Handbook

/aɪ/, /aʊ/ and /ɔɪ/ Word List

/aɪ/

Aisle
Buy
Bright
Decide
Died
Eye
Fight
Fine
Fly
Guy
Height
Heist
High
Idea
July
Lie
Light
Lime
Line
Mile
My
Pie
Sight
Sign
Sly
Tight
Time
Type
Whine
Why

/aʊ/

About
Allow
Bough
Bound
Bow
Brown
Clown
Couch
Count
Cow
Crowd
Doubt
Down
Drought
Fountain
Found
Frown
Gown
House
How
Howl
Loud
Meow
Mouth
Mouse
Now
Ouch
Out
Owl
Pound
Pout
Power
Prowl
Round
Shower
Sound
Tower
Town
Trout
Wow

/ɔɪ/

Ahoy
Alloy
Annoy
Avoid
Boil
Boy
Choice
Coin
Coy
Decoy
Destroy
Employ
Enjoy
Foil
Joint
Joy
Loyal
Moist
Noise
Oink
Oyster
Point
Rejoice
Royal
Soil
Soy
Spoil
Toilet
Toy
Turmoil
Voice
Voyage

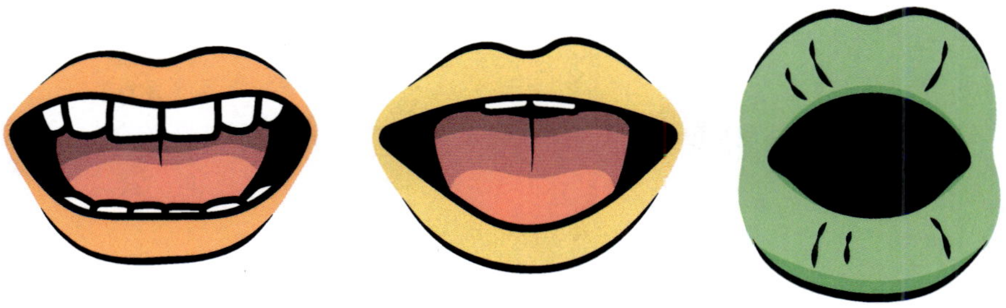

PEACHIE SPEECHIE'S

Speech Sound Handbook

Eliciting /aɪ/, /aʊ/ and /ɔɪ/

Eliciting Diphthongs

Diphthongs are combinations of sounds. Each diphthong has a starting position and an ending position. Clinicians can teach the first vowel as a starting point, and then guide them into the second vowel using successive approximations. Hand motions or touch cues can also be used.

Keep in mind that different regional dialects impact how vowels and diphthongs are pronounced. There may be some variation among your clients for this reason.

/aɪ/

This diphthong is a combination of the /a/ and /ɪ/ sounds. When combined, they sound a little different than they do individually.

Starting position:

- Lower your jaw.
- Lips open wide.
- Tongue tip low.
- Breathe out with your voice on.

Ending position:

- Raise your tongue and jaw.
- Spread your lips.

/aʊ/

This diphthong is a combination of the /a/ and /ʊ/ sounds. When combined, they sound a little different than they do individually.

Starting position:

- Lower your jaw.
- Lips open wide.
- Tongue tip low.
- Breathe out with your voice on.

Ending position:

- Raise your tongue.
- Move your lips into a rounded position.

/ɔɪ/

This diphthong is a combination of the /ɔ/ and /ɪ/ sounds. When combined, they sound a little different than they do individually.

Starting position:

- Round your lips.
- Pull your tongue back.
- Breathe out with your voice on.

Ending position:

- Pull your tongue up and forward.
- Spread your lips.

PEACHIE SPEECHIE'S

Speech Sound Handbook

Resources for your reading pleasure

Bauman-Wangler, J. (2008). *Articulatory and phonological impairments: A clinical focus.* (3rd ed.). Boston, MA: Pearson Education, Inc.

Bernthal, J., Bankston, N., & Flipsen, P. (2009). *Articulation and phonological disorders: Speech sound disorders in children.* (6th ed.). Boston, MA: Pearson Education, Inc.

Bleile, K. (2014). *The late eight.* (2nd ed.). San Diego, CA: Plural Publishing.

Crannell, K. (2000). *Voice and articulation* (4th ed.). Belmont, CA: Wadsworth/Thomson Learning.

Koch, C. (2019). *Motor-based treatment methods for speech sound disorders.* https://www.speechpathology.com/ask-the-experts/articulation-or-motor-based-approaches-20143

Passy, J. (2010). *Cued articulation: Consonants and vowels.* Victoria, Australia: Acer Press.

Rvachew, S. (1994). Speech perception training can facilitate sound production learning. *Journal of Speech Language and Hearing Research,* 37(2), 347-357.

Rusiewicz, H., & Rivera, J. (2017). The effect of hand gesture cues within the treatment of /r/ for a college-aged adult with persisting childhood apraxia of speech. *American Journal of Speech-Language Pathology,* 26, 1236-1243.

Secord, W., Boyce, S., Fox, R., Donohue, J., & Shine, R. (2007). *Eliciting sounds: Techniques and strategies for clinicians.* (2nd ed.). Clifton Park, NY: Delmar Cengage Learning.

Preston, J., Benway, N., Leece, M., Hitchcock, E., McAllister, T. (2020). Tutorial: Motor based treatment strategies for /r/ distortions. *Language, Speech and Hearing Services in Schools, 51,* 966-980.

Van Riper, C., & Emerick, L. (1990). Speech correction: *An introduction to speech pathology and audiology.* (8th ed.). Englewood Cliffs, NJ: Prentice-Hall, Inc.

Williams, A., McLeod, S., & McCauley, R. (2021). *Interventions for speech sound disorders in children.* (2nd ed.). Baltimore, MD: Paul H. Brookes Publishing Co.

PEACHIE SPEECHIE'S

Additional Resources

This Speech Sound Handbook pairs perfectly with our **"I Can Say..." workbooks!**

The "I Can Say..." workbooks provide clinicians with high quality visuals, engaging worksheets, and activities to do during therapy sessions!

Each workbook contains many opportunities for students to practice!

- Isolation
- Syllables
- Words
- Sentences
- Oral reading

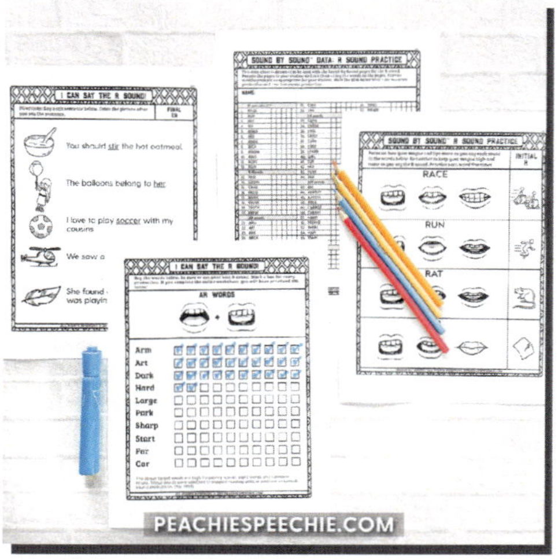

Scan this QR code to shop the collection!

SCAN ME

Examples from our book, I Can Say the R Sound

Thank you for shopping with Peachie Speechie. Use code **HANDBOOK** to get 10% off regular-priced items in your next order!

Peachie Speechie®

PEACHIE SPEECHIE'S

Additional Resources

Need help with the R sound?

Coarticulation for the R Sound

SCAN ME

R Sound Chaining

SCAN ME

I Can Say the R Sound

SCAN ME

Talk Like A Pirate Eliciting R

SCAN ME

Thank you for shopping with Peachie Speechie. Use code **HANDBOOK** to get 10% off regular-priced items in your next order!

Peachie Speechie®

Made in the USA
Middletown, DE
29 November 2023

44016863R00100